B·A·B·Y GIFTS

To Sew, Appliqué, Crochet and Knit

By Alison Wormleighton

Sedgewood ®Press

New York

Published by Sedgewood ® Press

For Sedgewood ® Press
Director Elizabeth P. Rice
Production Manager Bill Rose

Produced for Sedgewood ® Press by
Marshall Cavendish Books Limited
58 Old Compton Street
London W1V 5PA

For Marshall Cavendish
House Editor Dorothea Hall
Editor Alison Wormleighton
Designer Caroline Dewing
Production Craig Chubb

First printing 1988

ISBN 0-696-02304-0
Library of Congress Catalog Card
Number 87-062641

Typesetting by Litho Link Limited,
Welshpool, Powys
Printed in the United States of America

10 9 8 7 6 5 4 3 2 1

Picture credits
Barbara Bellingham: 29, 31.
Simon Butcher: 6, 23.
Steve Campbell: 91.
Bill Carter: 80, 83, 115.
Rod Delroy: 61, 63.
Ray Duns: 154, 157.
Fabbri: 138, 141.
John Garrett: 135.
Tony Hurley: 52, 53, 101.
Ron Kelly: 37.
Tom Leighton, 33, 34.
Di Lewis: 105, 107.
Nigel Messett: 47.
Ray Moller: 15, 16, 98, 100, 102,
    163.
Michael Newton: 94
Ian O'leary: 75, 76/7.
Roger Payling: 4.
Spike Powell: 9.
Peter Pugh Cook: 131.
Kim Sayer: 10, 39, 41, 43, 65, 67,
    68, 132/3.
Steve Tanner: 83, 85, 87.
Jerry Tubby: 27, 28, 58, 71.
Simon Wheeler: 5, 127, 129,
    166/7.
Victor Yuan: 145.

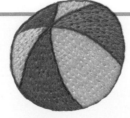

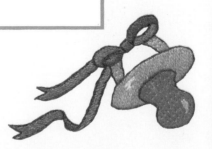

CONTENTS

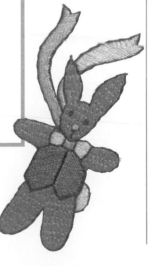

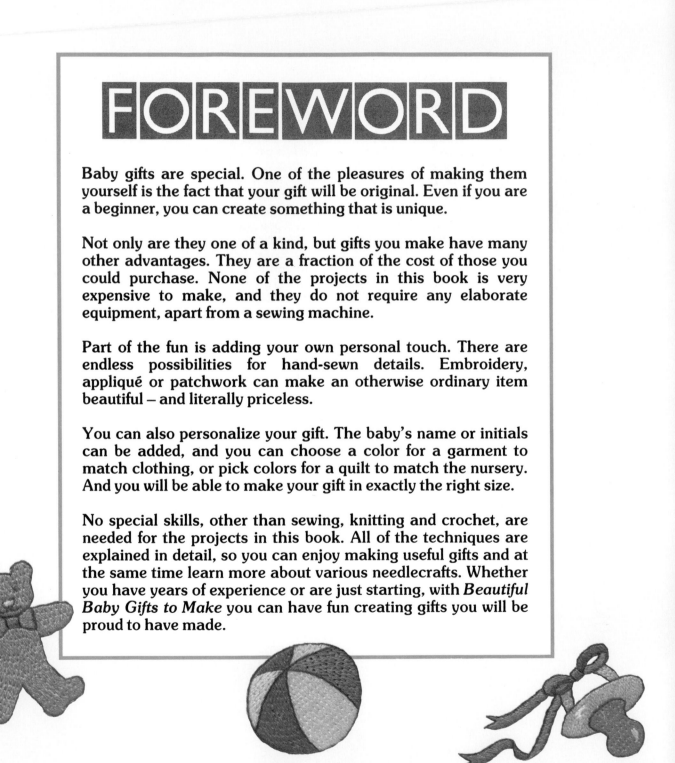

FOREWORD

Baby gifts are special. One of the pleasures of making them yourself is the fact that your gift will be original. Even if you are a beginner, you can create something that is unique.

Not only are they one of a kind, but gifts you make have many other advantages. They are a fraction of the cost of those you could purchase. None of the projects in this book is very expensive to make, and they do not require any elaborate equipment, apart from a sewing machine.

Part of the fun is adding your own personal touch. There are endless possibilities for hand-sewn details. Embroidery, appliqué or patchwork can make an otherwise ordinary item beautiful – and literally priceless.

You can also personalize your gift. The baby's name or initials can be added, and you can choose a color for a garment to match clothing, or pick colors for a quilt to match the nursery. And you will be able to make your gift in exactly the right size.

No special skills, other than sewing, knitting and crochet, are needed for the projects in this book. All of the techniques are explained in detail, so you can enjoy making useful gifts and at the same time learn more about various needlecrafts. Whether you have years of experience or are just starting, with *Beautiful Baby Gifts to Make* you can have fun creating gifts you will be proud to have made.

Before you begin

Graph patterns, where used, need to be enlarged to the correct size. To do this, you will need one or more sheets of dressmaker's pattern paper, a pencil, a ruler and (if the pattern has curved lines) a flexible curve. (This is a piece of plastic that can be molded into curves as a guide for drawing.) On the graph pattern you will find the scale to which it has been reduced, for example, 1 square = 2in. This determines how many squares of the pattern paper, with its full-size grid, equal one square on the graph pattern. Select a starting point on the pattern, note the location on the graph pattern grid and then mark the equivalent point on your full-size grid. To transfer straight lines, mark the next corner in the same way; then, using the ruler, draw a line between these two points. To transfer curved lines, mark the points on the full-size grid lines corresponding to the points where the pattern line crosses the lines of the small grid; after marking several points, join them using the flexible curve as a guide. Continue marking and joining points on the full-size grid to complete the pattern.

Knitting and crochet abbreviations
These abbreviations are used in all the knitting and crochet patterns in this book.

approx approximately
beg begin(ning)
ch chain(s)
cont continu(e) (ing)
dc double crochet
dec decreas(e) (ing)
foll follow(s) (ing)
in inch(es)
inc increas(e) (ing)
K knit
oz ounce(s)
P purl
pat(s) pattern(s)
psso pass slip stitch over

rem remain(s) (ing)
rep repeat(s) (ing)
RS right side(s)
sc single crochet
sl slip
sl st slip stitch
sp(s) space(s)
st(s) stitch(es)
st st stockinette stitch
tbl through back of loop(s)
tog together
WS wrong side(s)
yd yard(s)
yo yarn over hook or needle

NURSERY NEEDS

Furnishing the nursery is one of the delights of preparing for a new baby; this chapter contains many ways to make it comfortable, practical and cheerful.

Many parents prefer a small, cozy bassinet for their very young baby to sleep in. There are several different bassinet sets to choose from, with soft, padded bumpers and matching quilts. Once a baby has moved into a crib (usually at the age of one to four months), larger bumpers and quilts are needed. This size is ideal for appliquéd or machine-embroidered motifs, as in the quilts on pages 44, 46 and 51.

Baskets and holdalls are always useful for the many items which need to be within easy reach. There are two lined baskets included here: one a round, open basket with pockets (page 8) and the other a patchwork lined basket with a lid (page 10). Two handy holdalls are in this chapter, one knitted (page 10) and the other sewn (page 17). Both can be placed on a wall in the nursery and are invaluable for storing all kinds of baby gear. Also designed to be hung on the wall is a diaper holder (page 14), which looks pretty and holds folded diapers (or a baby's towels or sheets).

No nursery would be complete without at least one picture on the wall, and the unusual appliquéd picture on page 22 has bold, simple shapes and bright colors, which babies love.

7

LINED OPEN BASKET

You will need
For a round basket measuring 14½in across (45in circumference) by 6¾in deep
¾yd of 54in-wide fabric
1yd of ¼in-wide elastic
3¼yd of ½in-wide contrasting ribbon
1¼yd of contrasting bias binding
Thread

An open basket, lined with pretty fabric and full of deep pockets, is handy to keep near a baby's changing table.

For a first attempt choose a simply shaped basket. Because the lining will be washed frequently, a detachable lining is best. This one is held in place with ribbons tied at the handles.
⅜in seam allowances are included throughout unless otherwise specified.

Cutting out and preparation
To make pattern for base, stand basket on a sheet of brown paper or newspaper, and draw around outside edge. Cut out. This includes a ⅜in seam allowance. Then using this pattern, cut out one piece of fabric for base. For sides, cut out a rectangle 68in by 10in. For the pockets, cut out a second rectangle 68in by 8⅝in.
In side piece, cut a slot at each side as wide as the handle, and as deep as the handle plus 3in. Curve the lower edge of each slot, forming a U shape. Bind the slots with contrasting bias binding.

Making the pockets
Fold pocket section in half lengthwise and press. Stitch ⅜in from fold for elastic casing.
Divide pocket piece, minus the ⅜in seam allowance, into six equal parts and mark with pins then baste. Repeat on side piece. With right sides together, overlap bottom edges of pocket piece and side piece so that bottom edge of pocket piece is ¾in above bottom edge of side piece. Pin then stitch ⅜in from edge.
Thread elastic through casing at top of pocket piece, stitching ends to seam allowance. Fold pocket piece up over stitching; pin to lining, matching basting. Stitch along basting lines to form individual pockets.

Joining side piece and base
Fold side piece in half with right sides together, forming a ring, and join the short edges with a ⅜in seam. Press seam open.
Stitch one or two rows of gathering threads around bottom edge of side piece, ⅜in in from edge. Mark edges of side piece and base in four equal parts with a pin. Pull up gathers evenly, and knot gathering threads to hold gathers in place. With right sides together, pin base to side piece, matching pins. Stitch in place just outside gathering thread so that it will not show on right side. Trim and finish the seam.

Adding the ribbons
To make ribbon channels on the top edge, fold over ¼in and then ⅝in, and stitch along fold. Avoid stitching through the contrasting binding on the handle slots; hand sew across binding instead. Thread ribbons through channels, evening out the gathers that are formed. To prevent the ribbons from being pulled out, backstitch through channel halfway along each side. Fit lining into basket and tie in place.

LINED BASKET & LID

Line a small basket with patchwork fabric. It will hold many many baby things and look pretty in the nursery.

This patchwork fabric is made from hexagons, one of the easiest patchwork shapes used, but the principles described here can be adapted for a variety of patchwork formations. The patches are sewn together by hand, using paper patches which are removed upon completion.
⅜in seam allowances are included throughout unless otherwise specified.

Making the pattern
To make a hexagonal pattern, on the thin cardboard using pencil and compass, draw a circle with a 1in radius. With the compass still open at the same radius, place the compass point on the marked circle. Mark another point on the circle, 1in from the compass point. Move the compass point to this marked point and make another mark on the circle. Continue until the circle has been marked with six points. Join these points to give a six-sided figure, a hexagon. Carefully cut out the cardboard pattern.

Preparing the patches
Place this pattern on firm paper and mark around it. Cut out. Accuracy is most important at this stage.
Repeat to cut out about 70 paper patches.
Using cardboard as a guide, mark and cut out a selection of patches from five different print fabrics, adding ⅜in all around the pattern for the seam allowances. When cutting out each fabric patch, always align two parallel sides of the pattern with the straight grain of the fabric.
Next, cover the paper shapes with fabric patches by placing a paper patch in the center on the wrong side of fabric patch. Pin in position.
Fold over the ⅜in seam allowance along one side and baste through the paper patch and the fabric patch to hold. Carefully fold and turn the corner accurately, keeping the shape of the paper hexagon. Continue around, turning in all the edges.
Baste the seam allowances down, using a medium to large stitch. Do not fasten the thread firmly, as the basting has to be removed when the patchwork is complete. Do not iron the edges prior to basting – the soft, rounded edges are a feature of this type of patchwork. Care must also be taken that the fabric-covered patches are accurate and each side is of equal length, otherwise when sewn together they will not fit.

Sewing the patches together
Careful arrangement of patches is an important factor in making effective patchwork. Arrange a variety of patches together, to give an interesting pattern of color and print for the inside of the basket lid. The overall shape will not be a true oblong, due to the shape formed by the hexagons when they are sewn together, so part of the patchwork fabric will have to be cut.

You will need
One cane picnic basket 12in long, 10in wide and 7in deep
Two patchwork bag packs, from which we used five different print fabrics
⅞yd of 36in-wide plain fabric
White thread
Bias binding in matching or contrasting color
⅝yd of 36in-wide lightweight synthetic batting
Thin cardboard for hexagonal pattern
Firm paper for patches
Pencil and compass
Tracing paper
Invisible sewing thread
1⅜yd of ⅜in-wide elastic

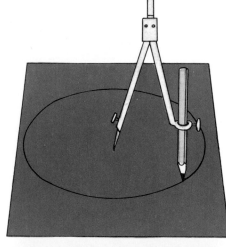

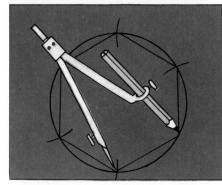

A hexagonal pattern is made using a compass and pencil to draw a circle and then divide the circumference into six equal segments.

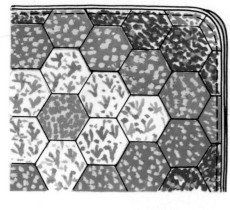

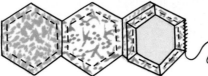

With this type of patchwork, fabric patches are folded over paper patches, basted and then sewn together by hand with right sides together before the paper patches are removed. The illustrations above show the basket lid lining and the decorative band that goes around the sides of the basket lining.

When the patches are arranged, take two of the adjoining patches and place with right sides together, matching all edges. Whipstitch along one of their common sides with white thread. Take neat, evenly spaced stitches and pick up only a small amount of the fabric edges with each stitch. Do not stitch through the papers.

Continue sewing the patches together in the same way, until you have sewn together enough to give a solid area of fabric, slightly larger than the lid of the basket. Remove all the basting stitches. Remove the paper patches and press from the wrong side.

Lining the lid

Place tracing paper on top of the basket lid. Mark and cut out a pattern the shape of the lid. Place the paper pattern of the lid in the center of your patchwork and pin in place. Cut out. Similarly, using the same tracing paper pattern, cut out one piece from batting and then cut out one piece from plain fabric for the lining.

Sandwich the batting between the patchwork and the plain lining. Pin and baste to hold the three layers together. Zig-zag stitch around the outer edge through all three layers.

Next, attach bias binding around the complete outer edge: open out one edge of the binding and, with right side of binding to right side of patchwork, match this edge of binding to the raw edge of the fabric; pin and baste along binding fold. Cut off excess binding and stitch narrow edges of binding together to fit. Stitch in place. Fold binding over raw edges to plain fabric side; pin and baste. Slip stitch binding neatly in place by hand.

Place fabric inside basket lid. Using invisible thread, hand sew the fabric to the basket around the bound edge of the patchwork.

Preparing the base lining

Place tracing paper inside base of basket. Mark and cut out a pattern the shape of the basket base. Using this pattern, cut out two pieces of plain fabric and one piece of batting.

Sandwich the batting between the two plain fabric pieces. Pin and baste to hold the three layers together. Zig-zag stitch around the outer edge of the base, through all three layers.

Preparing the side lining

Measure around the sides of the basket and the basket depth. From plain fabric cut one strip the combined length of all four sides plus ¾in seam allowance and twice the depth of the side plus ¾in seam allowance. Seam the strip if necessary, but try to make the seams coincide with the corners of the basket if possible. Fold the fabric strip in half lengthwise, wrong sides together, and press.

Cut a strip of batting ¾in shorter and half the width of the original fabric strip.

To make a decorative band of patchwork pieces, sew a number of patches together, matching opposite sides, to form a strip the same length as the plain fabric strip. Pin the patchwork strip on the plain fabric, ³/₈in below the center foldline. Slip stitch along the top edge of the patches. Slip stitch along the lower edge of patches.

Sandwich the batting strip in the folded strip of fabric. Pin and baste. Zigzag stitch along raw edges through all three layers.

Place strip inside basket and pin the two short ends together to fit correctly. Remove from basket, and pin, baste and stitch the seam. Press seam flat.

Assembling the basket lining

Pin and baste side lining to base lining, right sides together, taking care to produce neatly curved corners to match the shape of the basket. Place lining inside basket to achieve a good fit, adjusting the seam if necessary. Pin, baste and stitch seam. Remove all basting stitches. Place fabric lining inside basket. Using invisible thread, hand sew top edge of lining to the rim of the basket.

Making the elastic holding band

Cut a strip of elastic, long enough when unstretched to go around the four sides of the basket. Cut enough 1½in-wide strips of plain fabric to make, when joined together, one long strip which is twice the length of the elastic.

Fold the fabric strip in half lengthwise right sides together. Pin, baste and stitch along edge to form a ⁵/₈in-wide channel. Turn fabric channel right side out. Thread elastic through the fabric channel, pinning one end so that it does not slip inside the channel during threading.

Sew the two ends of elastic together firmly. Fold under a narrow seam allowance at one end of the fabric channel. Slip the other end of the fabric channel inside this end. Pin, baste and slip stitch ends together to finish, forming the holding band. Distribute the fullness of the gathers evenly.

Attaching the holding band

Pin the holding band to each corner of the basket, just under the row of patchwork. Pin again in the middle of each of the two long sides. Using invisible thread, sew the band in place, sewing through the elastic, the fabric lining and the basket, to make sure that it is firmly attached.

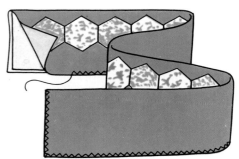

The decorative band that goes on the sides of the lining (above) is sewn onto a strip of plain fabric, which is then padded with batting. This forms the side of the basket lining and is sewn invisibly onto the basket (below left). An elasticized holding band is sewn on top (below right).

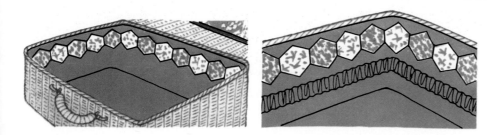

DIAPER HOLDER

A hanging holder for diapers keeps them close at hand and brightens the nursery. It's also useful for towels and bed linen.

Make the diaper holder from a crisp cotton fabric that will coordinate with the nursery décor. The holder is hung up with a plastic coat hanger. 5⁄8in seam allowances are included throughout unless otherwise specified.

Making and lining the main piece

Measure the size of a quarter-folded diaper – this will be the size of the completed base. The width of the main fabric piece should be twice the length of the base plus twice the width, less 1¾in. The length is 19in. From fabric, cut out one piece to these dimensions for holder.

Make up enough covered piping for both front edges: unfold bias binding and refold evenly in half around corded piping. Pin, baste and stitch down the complete length, using a piping foot or zipper foot on the machine. Stitch piping down front edge, with piping facing inward and stitching line 5⁄8in from edge. Stitch piping to opposite edge in same way. From fabric cut lining the same size as main piece. With right sides together, place lining on main piece. Stitch together down both front edges. Trim and turn right side out. Baste bottom raw edges of holder and lining together.

Making and lining the base

From fabric cut one base, adding 5⁄8in seam allowances all around. Mark center of one long edge. Stitch bottom edge of holder to base, each front 1½in from center mark.

From fabric cut out base lining the same size as base. Place lining and base fabric with right sides together. Pin, baste and stitch together around front and side edges. Trim around base and turn right side out. Turn in the back edges on base lining, enclosing raw edges. Pin, baste and slip stitch edges together by hand to finish.

Making the hanger piece

Place coat hanger on a piece of brown paper or newspaper. Make a pattern by drawing around hanger, adding ease on back and front, so hanger can be fitted inside the holder. Using pattern, cut two hanger pieces from fabric. Make a double ¼in hem at top opening edge of one hanger piece. Stitch hem. Repeat with second hanger piece.

Make a length of covered piping (as for front edges) long enough for base edge of hanger piece. Position piping along base edge of front hanger piece. Stitch in place.

Place hanger pieces with right sides together, matching raw edges. Stitch 5⁄8in seams, working from top opening around to base on each side.

Baste together top raw edges of main piece and lining. Pin top edges to hanger piece, matching piped fronts at center. Mark center backs on hanger and main piece and match together, to make excess fabric even at each side. After pleating the excess fabric at each side, fold the two

pleats in toward the front of the holder. Working from the inside, stitch
the hanger section to the main holder section with a ⅝in seam, using a
piping foot or a zipper foot on the machine.

Covering the cardboard base

From fabric cut out a cover for the cardboard base, making it twice the length of the cardboard base plus 3¼in, and the width of the base plus 1¼in. On one short side, turn under raw edge for ¼in then again for ¼in to form a double hem. Stitch hem in place. Fold base cover in half with right sides together and with hemmed edge 3in from opposite short raw edge. Stitch ⅝in seams. Trim and turn right side out. Fold under raw edges on remaining edges of flap to form double ⅜in hem. Miter corners and position the hem just under the hemmed edge. Pin, baste and stitch. From white cardboard, cut out one base piece: mark out the correct size with a set square. Then, using a metal ruler and very sharp craft knife, carefully cut out. Slot the cardboard base inside the base cover, then fold the hemmed edge inside the cover to close. Fit the fabric-covered cardboard base inside the holder. Insert the coat hanger.

FABRIC WALL HOLDALL

Help keep the nursery tidy with this stylish holdall made from coordinating fabrics.

This practical and attractive wall holdall is hung from a wooden pole with another pole across the base to support the shape. Most types of fabric will work, but the holdall must be strengthened with a very firm, extra-thick interfacing or the weight of the contents may pull the holdall out of shape.

Seam allowances vary and are specified throughout.

Cutting out

From check fabric cut a 25½in by 10¾in rectangle on the cross of fabric for front of pockets as shown in the cutting layout on page 19. From remaining fabric, cut the following 1½in-wide crosswise strips for binding edges: two 30in pieces for side edges and three 20in pieces for scallops. From the plain fabric, cut one rectangle 60in by 22in for front and back of holdall; and one 29½in by 10¾in for pocket lining.

From the extra-thick interfacing, cut one rectangle 21in by 22in to stiffen back of holdall; and two rectangles 10⅜in by 10¾in for the main pocket panels. From medium-weight interfacing cut a 25½in by 10¾in rectangle for pockets.

Stiffening the holdall

With wrong sides together and short edges even, fold the large plain rectangle in half and press in the fold. Open rectangle out with wrong side up and place the 21in by 22in piece of extra-thick interfacing on the lower half of fabric so the side edges are even, and the top and bottom edges of interfacing are 4¼in away from foldline and lower edge of fabric. Catchstitch interfacing to fabric across the width. This stiffened side will form the back of holdall.

Refold front half of holdall over back of holdall with interfacing sandwiched between and baste raw edges together. On front, baste a center line from top to bottom; and baste across 4¼in in from top to bottom level with the edges of the interfacing.

Cutting out and binding the scallops

Enlarge the graph pattern on this page for scallop shape to correct size and cut out in cardboard. Using dressmaker's chalk, draw around pattern to mark the scallop position at top fold edge: mark scallops at either side, each beginning 3⅛in in from sides, then the center one midway between. Stitch around scallops just outside the marked lines, then cut out scallops along chalk lines.

Fold and press ⅜in to wrong side along each long edge of the 1½in wide crosswise strips. With raw edges inside fold the strip in half again with the under half of strip just a little wider than the upper half.

With the wider half of binding underneath, sandwich the raw edge of scallops into binding, folding raw ends of binding in to finish them. Easing

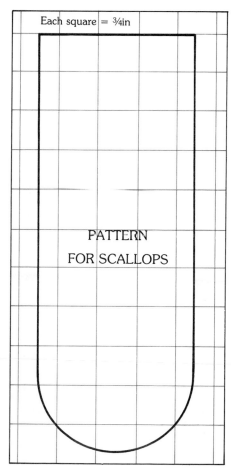

You will need

For a holdall measuring 22in by 24¾in

1⅝yd of 36in-wide plain fabric
¾yd of 60in-wide check fabric
¾yd of 32½in-wide extra-thick interfacing
⅜yd of 31½in-wide medium-weight interfacing
3yd of 1in-wide bias binding
Thread
Two 25in-long pieces of 1in wooden doweling or broom handles
Four screw-in knobs
Two pole brackets
Paint

Each square = ¾in

PATTERN FOR SCALLOPS

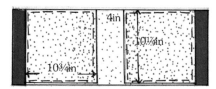

The scalloped top of the holdall is drawn with a cardboard pattern then cut out (top). The fabric has previously been stiffened with extra-thick interfacing. The pockets are also interfaced (above), using medium-weight interfacing.

the binding to lie flat around curves, pin, baste then topstitch binding in place near to fold, so that both edges of binding are caught with the same row of stitching.

Making the pockets

Lay out the plain pocket lining with the right side up. Place medium-weight interfacing on fabric with top and bottom edges even, and side edges 2in in from the fabric side edges. Pin, baste and stitch just inside the edge of the interfacing.

Place the two pieces of extra-thick interfacing on top of the medium-weight interfacing with the outer side edge and top edges even with edge of medium-weight interfacing, and a 4in space between edges of the extra-thick interfacing at the center. Baste in place around edges.

With right side up, lay checked pocket piece over the interfaced pocket lining so side edges are even with edges of interfacing. Baste around edges and down center of pocket. Baste to mark pleat crease lines 1in and 2in in from side edges and the same distances either side of center.

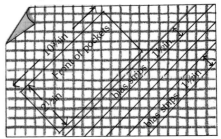

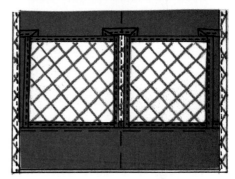

Cut two 30in lengths of purchased bias binding. Press binding in half and bind top and bottom edges of pocket as for scallops.

Form and press 1in deep pleats at both sides of interfaced pocket panels; the folds of center pleats should meet at the center basted line, and fold of side pleats should be even with side raw edges. Using the same method as before and turning ends under to finish, bind the four front creases of pleats with purchased bias binding.

With center matching, place the pocket section at the front of the holdall with the bottom edge of pockets even with basted line at lower edge of interfacing. Pin and baste the side edges of pocket gussets to side edges of holdall. Pin, baste and stitch pocket to front down the center of pocket between pleats. Folding raw ends under to finish, use crosswise strips to bind the side edges of holdall, enclosing side edges of pockets in the binding.

With the pleats formed, baste the lower edge of pockets to holdall along the line of binding stitching. Stitch along the same line.

Stitching casings

Fold 2½in over to back at top of each tab, and then baste in place across ends of tabs. Stitch across each tab just above the basting line marking the top of extra-thick interfacing. This will leave a casing in each of the tabs for the piece of doweling.

Zig-zag stitch lower edges of holdall together to finish. Fold 2¼in over to back along lower edge and baste in place near to zig-zag stitching. Stitch just below the basting line marking the lower edge of extra-thick interfacing, forming a casing for the top piece of doweling.

Finishing the holdall

Paint doweling and wooden knobs. When dry, insert doweling through the top and bottom casings. Thread brackets onto ends of top piece of doweling. Attach brackets to the wall.

Use firmly woven cottons (top left) for the holdall. Contrast a plain fabric with a color-coordinated print or check for pockets and bindings. These are cut on the cross, as shown in the cutting layout (top). After the edges of the pocket piece are bound, it is pleated, and the front creases are also bound (center). It is then sewn to the holdall, with the side edges being enclosed in the binding on the holdall side edges, and the center being stitched in place (bottom).

KNITTED WALL HOLDALL

The pockets on this knitted holdall are an ideal place for keeping a wide assortment of a baby's belongings.

Only the most basic knitting and sewing skills are needed to make this holdall. Worked in garter stitch, the holdall is begun at the bottom and knitted upward to the top. The large pocket is formed by turning the bottom up and stitching it to the front; to stop it from gaping, the center can be secured with an invisible seam or colored diaper pins. The holdall has a fabric backing and is trimmed with fabric strips.
A list of the abbreviations used is given on page 5.

Large pocket and front
Using A, cast on 56 sts. Work in garter st (K every row) in the foll stripe sequence: 12 rows A, 2 rows B, 2 rows C, 2 rows D, 55 rows A, * 2 rows D, 2 rows C, 2 rows B, 55 rows A, rep from * once, then work 2 rows D, 2 rows C, 2 rows B and 30 rows A.
Bind off.

Small pockets (make 4)
Using A, cast on 21 sts. Work in garter st stripe sequence as foll: 15 rows A, 2 rows D, 2 rows C, 2 rows B, 16 rows A. Bind off.

To finish
Fold bottom of front up 7in to RS. Join side seams using backstitch. Slipstitch small pockets in place.

Pocket bindings
Cut 5 strips of fabric 2½in wide and the length of each pocket plus ½in for seam allowance at each end. Attach RS of fabric strip to RS of pocket, ⅝in from top edge. Fold under seam allowance at both ends and fold strip over pocket edge. Slipstitch binding to inside of pocket.

Backing
Lay knitting on main fabric WS facing and baste tog. Cut fabric around knitting allowing an extra 1¼in along all sides. Hem top and bottom of fabric neatly and slipstitch fabric to knitting. Fold side edges over knitting. Tuck in raw edges. Pin, baste and stitch in place.

Doweling casing
Fold over 1in of top of knitting to WS and backstitch. Slot doweling through casing.

Cord
Using D, make a thick twisted cord as foll:
Cut 2 strands of yarn 80in long and knot tog 1in from ends. Fasten one end of the cord around a door or drawer handle. Holding the yarn taut, rotate until the strands are tightly twisted. Keeping the strands stretched out, fold in half at the center, letting the strands wrap tightly around one another. Knot the ends tog, leaving 4in between 2nd set of knots at one end and 4in to fold at other end, and approx 22in of cord at the center. Cut off the first set of knots at one end and clip along the fold at the other end. With the loose ends make a 2nd knot at each end 1in from the first. Trim tassel ends. Slot doweling into cord between knots at each end.

You will need
For a holdall measuring 16in wide by 25½in long
Bulky yarn:
16oz in main color A (white)
2oz in each of 3 contrasting colors B (fuchsia), C (rust) and D (dark maroon)
One pair of size 9 knitting needles
⅞yd of 36in-wide fabric
20in of ½in doweling
Thread

Gauge
14 sts and 28 rows to 4in over garter stitch worked on size 9 needles

APPLIQUÉD PICTURE

A baby's imagination will soar with this light, bright, airy picture hanging in the nursery.

This cheerful wall hanging is a combination of reverse and traditional appliqué techniques. The blue sky and the balloons are made by reverse appliqué; the clouds, baskets and mountains, plus the bar across the red balloon, are appliquéd on top.

⅛in seam allowances are included for the reverse appliqué, ¼in for the traditional appliqué and ⅜in for the binding.

Preparing to appliqué

Enlarge the design on page 25 (one square equals 2in) and then make patterns for all the different elements in the picture from thin cardboard. Place the cloud patterns on the wrong side of the pale blue fabric, and draw around them. Cut out, leaving a ¼in seam allowance all around each piece. (The pencil lines are the stitching lines.) In the same way, cut the mountains out of the two shades of green fabric, and the baskets out of the black fabric.

Cut a piece of sky blue fabric measuring 18in by 22in, and also cut the red, orange and yellow fabric the same size. Using the patterns, draw on the sky blue fabric the designs which are to be cut out of it (the balloon outlines) and those which are to be appliquéd on top (the clouds, baskets and mountains). Stack the fabrics together, with the yellow one at the bottom, then the orange, then the red, and the blue one on the top.

Pin all the layers together, starting at the center and pinning out to the edges. Baste ¼in outside the cutting lines (⅛in outside the sewing lines) around all the designs to be cut from the fabric. Make basting lines 1½in to 2in apart vertically and horizontally all over the remaining area of the top fabric (excluding the parts to be cut out).

Applying the balloons

Start with the balloons. Using embroidery scissors, carefully cut out the balloon outlines from the blue fabric, revealing the red layer underneath. Turn under ⅛in all around the balloon shapes and sew in place using an invisible hemming stitch. Use additional stitches at the corners, and catch in the yellow base fabric with every stitch.

On the red layer mark the balloon outline of the lefthand balloon and all the stripes of the righthand balloon. Baste and cut in the same way, revealing the orange layer. Cut out small pieces of green fabric and tuck them into the cut-out vertical stripes that are to be green on the righthand balloon. Turn under ⅛in along all raw edges and hand sew in place.

On the orange layer, mark all the stripes on the lefthand balloon, and the vertical stripes and horizontal bars that are to be yellow on the righthand balloon. Baste and cut out, revealing the yellow base layer. Tuck small pieces of red and green fabric into the appropriate stripes of the lefthand balloon. Turn under ⅛in along all raw edges and hand sew in place.

For the horizontal green and red bars across the center of the righthand

You will need

For a picture measuring 18in by 22in
45in-wide cotton fabric as follows:
¾yd each of red, orange, sky blue and yellow
¼yd each of dark green and emerald green
⅛yd of pale blue
Scrap of black
Thread
Thin cardboard

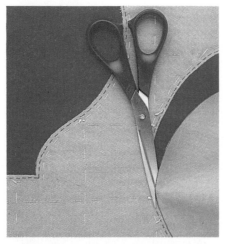

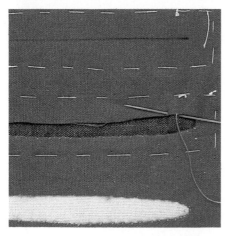

With reverse appliqué (top), only one layer at a time is cut away and sewn in place. Colors not already in the pile can be added by inserting a small piece of fabric into the cut-out design (above). The edges are then rolled under and sewn in the normal way.

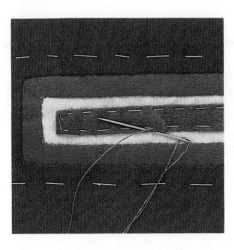

Motifs can easily be added to a reverse appliqué design. A pattern is used to cut out the fabric, with a small seam allowance all around, which is turned under and basted. The piece is then basted in place and finally sewn down with blind-stitch through all layers of fabric.

balloon, cut out from separate fabric, allowing a ¼in seam allowance all around. Turn under the edges and baste, then place the bars in position and baste. Blind-stitch through all layers.

Applying the remaining motifs

Sew a gathering thread halfway between the pencil line and the cut edge on the convex curves (clouds and mountaintops), using very short stitches. Cut small notches in the seam allowance to remove any surplus fullness. Clip all concave curves (valleys between mountains) halfway to the seam line. Turn under the edges of all pieces along the seam line and baste. Pull the gathering threads on the convex curves slightly before basting.

Pin the clouds in position on the blue background fabric, and baste ¼in from the edge. Sew on the clouds with a very tiny blind-stitch, then carefully cut away the background fabric underneath each cloud with embroidery scissors, leaving a ¼in seam. Repeat the procedure for the baskets, then the mountains in the distance, and finally the mountains in the foreground.

Binding the edges

From the sky blue fabric, cut one strip measuring 1½in by 18in (for the top edge) and the two pieces measuring 1½in by 23½in for the sides. Also cut four pieces of sky blue fabric measuring 2½in by 4¾in for the hangers. Cut a strip of emerald green fabric measuring 1½in by 18in for the bottom border.

Place the top and bottom border strips in position on the picture with right sides together and raw edges even, and stitch ⅜in seams.

Next prepare the hangers. Fold each of the hanger pieces in half lengthwise, with right sides together, and stitch a ¼in seam down the long edge. Turn the pieces right side out and press them flat, with the seam running down the middle. Fold the pieces in half and position them evenly along the top edge of the work. They should be placed on the back of the work, lying flat with their raw edges matching the raw top edge. (They will be turned up when the binding is complete.) Sew the hangers to the picture, stitching on the seam made when adding the binding strip.

Next prepare the side strips. To continue the design onto the binding, measure the height of the relevant motifs ⅜in in from the raw edge and cut pieces of matching fabric to the width of the strip and to the measured height of the motif, plus seam allowances. Sew them to the side strips at the appropriate points, making sure that the extra pieces follow the curve of the existing motifs. Cut away the strip underneath, as before.

Sew the side binding strips to the picture and to the top and bottom strips, which should be held out flat. Next turn under ⅜in all around the raw edge of the binding and turn the binding to the back of the picture. Blind-stitch the binding in place at the back, then turn the hangers up and blind-stitch them up to the edge of the picture and across the top.

1 sq = 2in

BASSINET LINING & COVER

You will need
Quilted fabric
Unquilted fabric in the same design
¼in-wide elastic
Medium-weight batting
Thread

A lined wicker bassinet gives a new baby somewhere cozy to sleep, and a lining using ready-quilted fabric is easy to make.

A quilted lining not only gives the baby extra protection from the basketwork but is also a good way to make a bassinet fit into your color scheme. This lining is made from ready-quilted fabric and is held in place with an elasticized casing, which grips the bassinet underneath the top lip. A simple ruffle gives the bassinet a soft look. The cover is made from matching unquilted fabric, and trimmed with a ruffle near the top edge. ⅜in seam allowances are included throughout unless otherwise specified.

Making the lining
Measure the length and width of the outside of the bassinet base between the widest points. From quilted fabric, cut out a rectangle of fabric for base. Place bassinet on wrong side of quilted fabric and mark around. Remove bassinet and cut out base around marked line. (The width of the bassinet base will provide the seam allowance around the base, so extra will not be needed.)
Mark one side center on bassinet lip. Measure from this point around the bassinet along the lip; divide into three sections and mark. Add ¾in for seam allowances to each piece. Measure depth, and add 5in. Make a paper pattern of each section. From quilted fabric, cut side sections, adding 4¾in to top edge for the elasticized casing to grip bassinet lip. Finish side edges and pin pieces together.
Baste and stitch the three side sections together in the correct order, with ⅜in seams, to form a ring for the complete side section.
Run a line of gathers along the base edge of side piece, starting and ending at seams. Divide outer edge of bassinet base into three. Pull up gathers evenly to fit each base section. Pin, baste and stitch side piece to base, matching seams with marks on outer edge of base. Trim seam allowance and finish all the edges together with zig-zag stitch.
Finish top edge of lining with zig-zag stitches. Turn down ¾in along top edge to form casing for elastic. Stitch around casing, leaving an opening at one seam to insert elastic.

Making and attaching the ruffle
From unquilted fabric cut out six fabric widths for ruffle, each 8in deep. Pin, baste and stitch ruffle pieces together to form a ring with ⅜in seams. Turn under ¼in on base edge of ruffle; turn under a further ¼in to form a double hem. Pin, baste and stitch double hem in place around base edge of ruffle. Turn down 1¾in along top edge of ruffle; turn under ¼in on raw edge. Run two rows of gathering stitches around ruffle top, 1⅛in and 1¼in from top folded edge.
Place lining inside bassinet, folding over top edge. Mark ruffle position on lining.
Remove lining and pin ruffle on lining in marked position, pulling up gathers to fit. Stitch through center of gathering stitches.

Making the elasticized top

Cut off a piece of elastic, measuring around the bassinet under lip and slightly stretching elastic to allow for a good grip. Thread elastic through casing. Position lining inside bassinet. Pull up elastic until lining fits under top lip of bassinet. Stitch elastic together, then stitch opening closed.

Making the cover

The length of the cover should be about two-thirds the length of the bassinet, plus an allowance for tucking it in at the bottom. The width should be the same as the bassinet, plus extra for tucking in. From unquilted fabric cut out two cover pieces. Cut out and make up a 3in-deep single ruffle as long as the width of the cover.

27

Position the ruffle along one short edge, with the wrong side of the ruffle facing the right side of the cover and with raw edges even. Pin and baste in place. Place the other cover piece on top, right sides together and raw edges even, sandwiching the ruffle between the two layers. Pin, baste and stitch along this short edge with a ⅜in seam.

Pin, baste and stitch the two cover pieces together along the other short edge, right sides together, with a ⅜in seam; leave a 5½in opening in the center of the seam.

Holding the cover like a ring, wrong side out, crease the fabric 3in away from each seam and parallel to it. Lay the fabric flat again, with the folds at each end and the seams 3in away from them. Position the batting on one side. With right sides together, machine stitch both sides with ⅜in seams.

Trim the side seams and turn the cover right side out through the back opening. Turn under the opening edges in line with the seam, and slip stitch neatly together.

APPLIQUÉD BASSINET SET

Celebrate a birthday with bunches of pastel-colored balloons that turn a bassinet set into a daily celebration.

This charming bassinet quilt and pillowslip feature an appliquéd motif which is first bonded to the fabric then zig-zagged in place. The quilt consists of two layers of silky polyester fabric, with a layer of batting and a layer of lining fabric in between. The appliqué is worked through the top layer of polyester, the batting and the lining. The appliqué on the pillowslip is worked through the top layer of polyester and a layer of muslin; the edges of the appliqué are given a raised, quilted effect with strands of yarn threaded through channels on the underside of the fabric. The pillowslip is designed to take a baby's safety pillow. A baby less than one year old can be supported by a pillow but should not sleep on one. ⅝in seam allowances are included throughout unless otherwise specified.

Cutting out

Cut two 19¾in by 26in rectangles from white polyester for the quilt, and one each 14¼in by 22in, 14¼in by 19¾in and 4¾in by 14¼in for the pillowslip.

Cut the remaining white fabric into 4¼in-wide strips and join to make a 14ft length for the quilt ruffle and a 3½yd length for the pillowslip ruffle.

Cut one piece each of lining and batting 19¾in by 26in for the quilt, and one lining 14¼in by 19¾in for the pillowslip.

Making the quilt

Trace the balloon and bow shapes which are shown on page 30 and use to cut cardboard patterns.

You will need

For a quilt measuring 21½in by 27¾in and a pillowslip 21½in by 16in
2¼yd of 45in-wide white silky polyester
⅝yd of 45in-wide white lining fabric
20in by 27½in piece of polyester batting
⅝yd of 15in-wide transfer fusing web
14¼in by 19¾in piece of white muslin
6in squares of pink, blue, green, peach and lilac polyester
Thread
Scraps of white worsted weight yarn
Bodkin
Thin cardboard

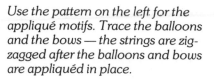

Use the pattern on the left for the appliqué motifs. Trace the balloons and the bows — the strings are zig-zagged after the balloons and bows are appliquéd in place.

Fuse transfer fusing web to the wrong side of the colored fabrics, and cut two balloons from each color and five bow shapes from the peach fabric. Fuse the balloons to the right side of one piece of polyester.

Sandwich the batting between the appliquéd fabric and the lining. Baste. Using matching thread and a closely spaced zig-zag stitch, appliqué balloon pieces into place, adding zig-zagged "strings." Fuse bows over the strings.

Press the 14ft ruffle strip in half lengthwise, wrong sides together, and gather the raw edges of the strip. Fit the ruffle around the edge of the quilt on the right side, adjusting gathers to fit; pin and then baste in place, turning in the raw ends and slip stitching neatly.

Place the quilt and the second piece of polyester, which forms the backing fabric, right sides together. Leaving a gap for turning right side out, stitch the fabrics together all around with a ⅝in seam, catching the ruffle in the seam. Turn the quilt right side out and slip stitch the opening closed.

Making the pillowslip
Cut four balloons and one bow from the colored fabrics, and fuse to the right side of the 14¼in by 19¾in piece of polyester. Baste the muslin to the wrong side of the polyester, and appliqué the balloons, strings and bows as for the quilt.

Machine stitch around the balloon edges, ¼in outside the zig-zagged edges. Using a bodkin, thread these channels with strands of yarn for a raised, quilted effect.

Baste the lining to the wrong side. Make a ruffle from the 3½yd length and stitch in place, as for the quilt.

Hem one long edge of the 4¾in by 14¼in piece of polyester and stitch to the right hand edge of the appliquéd fabric, right sides together. Hem one short edge of the 14¼in by 22in piece of polyester. Turn back the hemmed edge of this piece to match the pillowslip front. With right sides together, sew the pillowslip front and back together along the top, bottom and lefthand edges. Turn the pillowslip right side out.

You will need
3⅞yd of 48in-wide printed cotton fabric
4½yd of 36in-wide plain cotton fabric
2⅝yd of 36in-wide lightweight batting
2¼yd of elastic
10yd of ¼in-wide ribbon
Small bunch of fabric flowers
Thread
Snaps

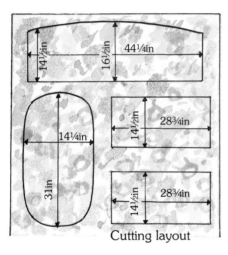

Cutting layout

The yardages shown at the top are for a bumper and quilt cover with the above dimensions, to fit an average-size bassinet. To make them larger or smaller, measure the bassinet as described on this page and adjust the yardages accordingly.

Use a pretty printed cotton to machine quilt a bumper for a bassinet, then make a coordinating quilt cover.

Quilting fabric yourself gives you a wide choice of prints and colors and you can adjust the thickness of the batting if you would prefer a thicker bumper for the bassinet. Made from a printed cotton fabric in soft pastels, this quilted bumper is finished with a ruffle, ribbon and matching fabric flowers. The quilt cover is made from coordinating plain fabric and has a matching patterned ruffle. The corners are trimmed with ribbon and fabric flowers to match the bumper.
⅝in seam allowances are included throughout unless otherwise specified.

Making the pattern and cutting out the bumper
Place the base of the bassinet on a piece of brown paper or newspaper and trace the outline. Remove the bassinet and cut out the pattern. This will allow you a ⅝in seam allowance. Measure around the lip of the bassinet and then the height of the bassinet sides at the top, side and bottom. Draw a paper pattern from the center of one side around the top to the center of the opposite side. Draw a second pattern from the center of one side to the center of the bottom; cut out the two pattern pieces.
From the printed fabric cut out one base (which already includes a seam allowance) plus one top piece and two bottom side pieces (adding 1¼in seam allowance to the upper edges and ⅝in seam allowance to lower and side edges). Repeat for the batting and plain fabric.

Quilting and assembling the bumper
Place the batting base on the wrong side of the patterned fabric base, matching raw edges. Pin and baste the layers together vertically and horizontally at 4in intervals, working from the center outward and beginning all parallel lines from the same side.
Mark out diagonal quilting lines 2in apart and at right angles to each other. Again starting at the center, quilt the layers together by machine.
Place one bottom side piece and the top piece with right sides together and side edges matching. Pin, baste and stitch together with a ⅝in seam. Repeat with second bottom side piece.
Place the corresponding batting pieces on the wrong side of the joined top and bottom fabric pieces, overlapping the seam allowances. Baste and quilt together as with the base.
Place the bottom side pieces with right sides together; pin, baste and stitch the bottom seam, making a ⅝in seam.
Run two rows of gathering stitches ⅝in from the lower edge of the quilted side piece. Position the quilted base on the quilted side piece with right sides together, pulling up the gathers so that the side piece will fit around the base. Pin, baste and stitch together.

Making the lining
Pin, baste and stitch the plain fabric side pieces and base together in the

same way. Place the plain fabric on the quilted piece with wrong sides together, matching seams and outer edges. Turn the top edges together to the wrong side to form a double ⅝in wide casing. Pin, baste and stitch in place, leaving a short opening. Thread elastic through the casing; overlap elastic edges and stitch together firmly. Slip stitch to close.

Completing the bumper

For the ruffle, cut six 8in wide strips across the fabric width. Pin, baste and stitch the strips together with narrow French seams. Turn under a narrow double hem at the lower edge of the ruffle; pin, baste and stitch in place. Turn under 1½in on the opposite edge; pin and baste.

Divide the ruffle into four equal sections. Divide the quilted bumper into four equal sections. Run two rows of gathering stitches through the double fabric 1¼in and just under 1½in from folded top edge, stitching each section in turn. Position the wrong side of the ruffle on the right side of the bumper with the gathering stitches 1⅛in from casing edge. Pull up the gathers in each section in turn to fit. Pin, baste and stitch the ruffle in place between the rows of gathering stitches.

Once the base and side piece are quilted, they are sewn together. The side piece is gathered at the lower edge and stitched along this edge to the base.

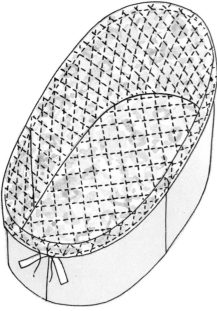

Position ribbon around the ruffle over the gathering stitches; hand-sew in place. Make six bows, snipping the ends into V-shapes. Sew to the bassinet at the sides, adding a fabric flower to each bow.

Cutting out and sewing the quilt cover

From plain fabric, cut out two pieces each 31in by 28¾in. For the ruffle, cut out five 4in wide strips across the width of the patterned fabric.

Fold a 1in wide double hem along one short edge of one fabric piece for the opening at the lower edge. Pin, baste and stitch hem in place.

On the other main piece, place two lengths of ribbon diagonally across the upper two corners; baste and stitch in place. Stitch two lengths of ribbon across each of the remaining corners, tie ribbons into bows at the center and add two fabric flowers to each bow.

Pin and stitch the ruffle strips together into a ring with narrow French seams. Fold ruffle in half lengthwise with wrong sides together. Divide the ruffle into four equal sections. Run a double row of gathering stitches, ⅝in from raw edges, on each section in turn. Pull up each ruffle section and with right sides together and raw edges matching, pin to the unhemmed main piece. At the lower edge arrange the ruffle so that it is 2in from the edge. Stitch the ruffle to the cover.

Fold a 1in wide double hem at the short edge so that it covers the raw edges of the ruffle; pin, baste and stitch in place.

Place the second main piece on the first with right sides together, raw edges matching and ruffle in between. Pin, baste and stitch around the cover, beginning 6in in from one side edge, stitching along the hem, all around to 6in in from the opposite side edge. Zig-zag stitch raw edges together to finish. Stitch across the double hem at the lower edge, at each side of the opening. Sew snaps into opening. Turn cover right side out.

Use a pretty floral print for the bumper and a coordinating plain fabric for the quilt cover (bottom). The quilt cover (below) is made from two pieces of fabric sewn together with right sides together, with the ruffle sandwiched between. A hemmed opening is left at one end for inserting the quilt, and snaps are sewn on so it can be closed.

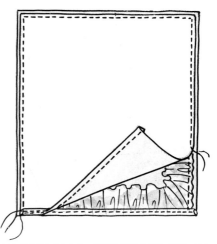

35

BASSINET BEDDING SET

Make a pretty bedding set from mix and match sheets for baby's first bed: bumpers, quilts, sheets and mattress cover.

The set consists of two sheets and two quilts (to provide a clean set when the other set is being washed), quilted bumpers for all four sides of the bassinet, and a mattress cover.

Seam allowances vary and are specified throughout.

Making the bumper

Cut out side and end pieces for bumper from mini floral sheeting, following the cutting layout on page 38. From batting cut out two pieces each 30in by 10in for side pieces and two pieces each 15in by 10in for end pieces.

Place batting side piece in between two fabric side pieces, matching outer edges and with right sides on the outside. Pin and baste together, taking large stitches. Work lines of diagonal stitching across the side piece, through all three thicknesses, spacing the lines of stitching 2in apart. Sew lines of diagonal stitching across the side piece, at right angles to the first rows of stitching, to form a quilted diamond effect. Make up the second side piece and the end pieces in the same way.

For ties, cut out eight 12in lengths from bias binding. On one tie piece, fold one short edge in ⅜in and baste. Fold the tie piece in half lengthwise, wrong sides together. Baste and stitch together down entire length. Make up seven more ties in the same way. Position raw short edge of one tie in the center of each short side of each bumper piece. Pin and baste in place with tie facing in toward center of piece.

Pin, baste and stitch one side of bias binding all around the outer edge of side piece, with right sides together and raw edges even, catching in ends of ties. Miter the corners and join the short edges of bias binding together to fit. Fold binding over the outer edge; pin, baste and slip stitch to the stitch line on the opposite side. Bind the outer edge of second side piece and the outer edge of both end pieces in the same way. Position the bumper inside the bassinet, tying the ties in each corner.

Making the sheets

To make one sheet, cut out one piece from floral sheeting, following the cutting layout on page 38. These measurements include seam allowance. Make a double hem all around the edge of the sheet by turning under ⅜in and then ¾in. Pin and baste in place, mitering the corners. Stitch in position. Repeat for the second sheet.

Making the mattress cover

For mattress cover, cut out one piece 71in by 20in from plain sheeting. On each short side of the mattress cover make a double hem by turning under ⅜in and then ¾in. Pin, baste and stitch both the hems in position. To form tuck-in piece, measure 30in in from one short side and pin to mark. Fold fabric at this mark, wrong sides together. Fold the 8¾in of

You will need

For a bassinet 15in wide, 30in long and 10in deep, measured on the inside of the bassinet
1⅛yd of 90in-wide floral sheeting
⅝yd of 90in-wide mini floral sheeting, for set of bumpers
⅝yd of 90in-wide plain sheeting, for mattress cover
1½yd of 36in-wide medium-weight batting
13¾yd of ½in-wide bias binding
Thread

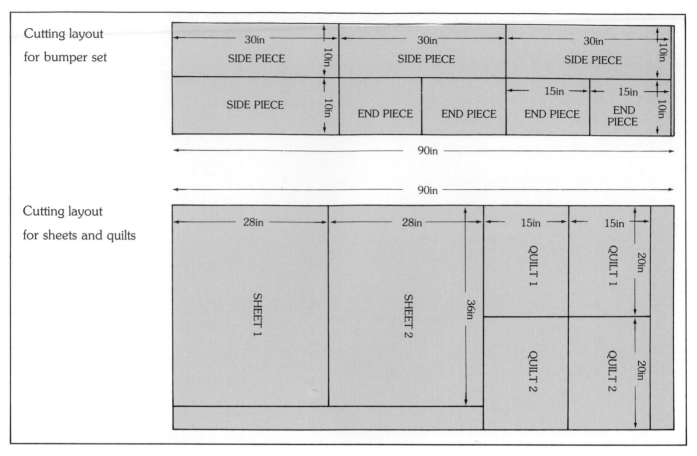

Cutting layout for bumper set

30in	30in	30in	10in
SIDE PIECE	SIDE PIECE	SIDE PIECE	10in

| SIDE PIECE | END PIECE | END PIECE | 15in END PIECE | 15in END PIECE | 10in |

10in

90in

Cutting layout for sheets and quilts

90in

28in	28in	15in	15in	20in
SHEET 1	SHEET 2 (36in)	QUILT 1	QUILT 1	20in
		QUILT 2	QUILT 2	20in

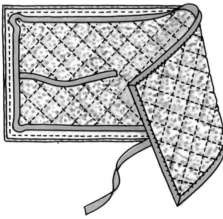

The edges of the bumper are bound with bias binding, catching in the ends of the ties in the seam.

excess fabric inside. Pin, baste and stitch a ³⁄₈in seam down each long side. Refold the mattress cover wrong side out. Pin, baste and stitch a ³⁄₄in seam down each long side. Turn cover right side out.

Making the quilts

To make one quilt, cut out two quilt pieces from floral sheeting, following cutting layout above. From batting cut out one piece 20in by 15in.

Place batting piece between the two fabric pieces, matching all outer edges and with right sides on the outside. Pin and baste together. Stitch diagonally across the fabric through all thicknesses in parallel lines 2in apart. Now stitch diagonally across the fabric in parallel lines 2in apart at right angles to the first rows of stitching, to form a quilted diamond effect.

Pin and baste one side of the bias binding all around the outer edge of quilt, with right sides together and raw edges even. Miter the corners and sew the short edges of bias binding together to fit. Stitch the first side of the bias binding in position. Fold the bias binding over the outer edge of the quilt; baste and slip stitch the remaining edge of the bias binding to the stitching line on the opposite side.

Repeat for the second quilt.

HALF-HEIGHT CRIB BUMPER

A half-height crib bumper with ruffle trim and quilted effect is a pretty way to protect a young baby from drafts.

Crib bumpers protect a baby from cold drafts and from bumps to head and limbs from the crib slats. This half-height bumper – which consists of rectangles of soft, lightweight batting sandwiched between two layers of fabric – is trimmed around the top and sides with a matching ruffle. The padding is anchored in place with French knots, giving an attractive cushioned appearance. Fabric ties hold the bumper in position on the

You will need
Cotton or other firm, washable fabric
Medium-weight synthetic batting
Thread
Stranded embroidery thread (one shade darker than background fabric if pastel)

Two bumpers can be used together (opposite) to fit around the entire crib. This is especially useful for babies who move around a lot in their sleep, as it will help keep them cozy and comfortable all night long. And because the bumper is relatively low, the baby can still see over the top, so that they will not feel too confined.

crib slats. The bumper fits around the head end of the crib, extending halfway down the sides. If you wish, you can make two half-height bumpers to fit around the entire crib, as in the photograph.

⅝in seam allowances are included throughout unless otherwise specified.

Making the main piece

Measure around the crib from the center slat on one long side to the center slat on the opposite long side. This will be the length of the bumper. Measure the height from the mattress, but only to between a half and two-thirds of the crib height, taking ruffle depth of 1¼in into account. This will be the height of the bumper. Add 1¼in to each measurement for seam allowances, then cut out two pieces of fabric and one piece of batting to the required size. Position batting on the wrong side of one fabric piece; pin and baste together around the outer edge.

Making the ruffle

Measure one long edge and both short edges. Cut fabric strips 3½in wide on the bias, and sew together to make double this length. Sew short edges of fabric strips together to make a ring. Fold in half lengthwise, wrong sides together. Stitch two rows of gathering stitches through both fabric layers. Pull up gathers.

Making and attaching the ties

For the ties, measure around a crib slat and add enough to form bows when the two ends are tied together. From fabric cut six ties to this length, by 1¼in wide. On each tie turn under ¼in on all edges. Fold in half lengthwise, wrong sides together. Pin, baste and topstitch.

Fold one tie in half and position folded center of tie on one short edge of bumper, 4in from base edge. Pin and baste ties in place. Repeat, to position ties on the opposite short edge. Position two remaining ties at top edge on the corner seamlines. If the crib has a solid end, position each corner tie so it can be fitted around the last slat on each long side. Pin and baste the ties in place.

Attaching the ruffle

Position ruffle along both short sides and top edge of padded piece, with right sides together and raw edges matching. Pin, baste and stitch to bumper, catching in the ties.

Finishing the bumper

Position remaining fabric piece with right side facing padded piece, matching outer edges. Pin, baste and stitch together all around with a ⅝in seam; leave opening in base. Trim and turn right side out. Turn under opening edges and slip stitch together.

Work French knots (see page 44) on both sides of the bumper, using six strands of embroidery thread and pulling taut between the two sides to get the buttoned effect.

FULL-HEIGHT CRIB BUMPER

You will need
Cotton or other firm, washable fabric
Medium-weight batting
1in-wide bias binding
Thread

An active older baby will benefit from the extra comfort of a full-height padded lining for his or her crib.

This full-height crib bumper features lengthwise quilting plus contrasting binding and ties. It reaches all the way from the top of the crib to the base, with the mattress helping to anchor the bumper in place.
⅝in seam allowances are included throughout unless otherwise specified.

Cutting out
Measure the crib to figure out the dimensions of each piece. For width of each side section, measure from center slat to corner slat on one long side; for height, remove mattress and measure from base to top bar. Add 1¼in to each measurement for seam allowances. For width of head section, measure across one end, from corner to corner, and add 1¼in for seam allowances; the height will be the same as the side pieces.
Cut out four side pieces and two head pieces. When using a one-way print fabric, cut out the pieces so that the top of the pattern is at the top of the crib. If using a plain or small allover print fabric, the bumper can be cut all in one piece, omitting the corner seams.
For the batting, measure around crib from center slat on one long side to opposite center slat. Cut out one piece.

Making the main piece
Stitch one head piece in between two side pieces with ⅝in seams. Repeat for other head piece and side pieces.
Sandwich batting in between fabric pieces. Baste through padded piece around outer edge and across fabric every 4in. Pin, then quilt vertical lines at 3in intervals, beginning in the center of the head section.

Making and attaching the ties
For ties cut six 27in pieces of binding. Fold each piece in half lengthwise, wrong sides together, turning under ¼in at raw edges. Pin and topstitch along long and short edges.
Fold one tie in half and position folded center of tie on one short edge, 4in from base edge. Repeat, to position second tie at top of short edge. Pin and baste ties in place. Repeat, to position ties on the opposite short edge. Position two remaining ties at top edge on the corner seamlines. Pin and baste the ties in place.

Binding the edges
With right sides together, stitch one long edge of bias binding around outer edge of bumper, catching the ties in at sides and top edge, and stitching short edges together. To prevent the binding from stretching, sew it together at the center of the base edge with a plain flat seam on the straight grain. Fold binding over the raw edges of the bumper to the opposite side, folding neat miters on each corner. Slip stitch binding in place over previous stitches.

EMBROIDERED CRIB QUILT

You will need
For a quilt measuring approximately 25in by 36in
1½yd of 36in-wide plain-colored cotton lawn
⅜yd of 36in-wide patterned lawn
⅝yd each of 36in-wide cream satin and lining fabric
Thread
1⅜yd of 36in-wide 4oz polyester batting
Machine embroidery thread in red and gray plus two shades each of green and brown
Stranded embroidery thread in red, yellow, blue, green and pink

Create an idyllic scene for an infant to wake up to with this beautiful embroidered crib quilt.

In this quilt six panels of satin are each quilted with machine embroidery featuring the same motif and surrounded by a border of plain lawn fabric. The edges of the quilt are bound with patterned lawn. A medium-sized, machine-embroidered straight stitch and hand-embroidered French knots are used, but you could adapt this idea to your own design, utilizing different stitches. The size of the quilt could also be adjusted to suit the crib dimensions.
⅜in seam allowances are included throughout unless otherwise specified.

Cutting out the panels
Cut six 9¾in squares from satin and six from the lining fabric. Cut one 26in by 37in piece and six 9¾in squares from batting.

Preparing the panels
Enlarge the house pattern from the graph pattern opposite, and, using dressmaker's carbon paper, transfer the pattern to the right side of the satin squares. Pin and baste each piece of satin to a square of batting and lining fabric.

Embroidering the design
Using a medium-sized straight stitch and thread in the colors shown, machine embroider the house design on each panel. Using two strands of embroidery thread in the colors shown, hand embroider French knots as flowers at the front of each cottage.

Assembling the quilt
Cut the plain-colored lawn into one 37in by 26in piece, three 37in by 2¾in strips and four 26in by 2¾in strips. With right sides together, pin, baste and stitch the quilted panels to the plain border strips with ⅜in seams. Pin and baste the quilt top to a piece of batting cut to size and the 26in by 37in piece of plain cotton lawn.

Topstitching the quilt
Using a straight stitch and matching thread, and working through all layers of fabric, topstitch around each square panel of the quilt, continuing the lines of stitching over the border strips.

Binding the edges
Cut and sew together the patterned lawn to make two 37in by 2⅛in strips and two 26in by 2⅛in strips. With right sides together, stitch a strip of patterned binding along each side of the quilt with ⅜in seams. Fold the patterned binding over the raw edges of the quilt, turn under ⅜in and catchstitch to the backing fabric. Turn under and catchstitch the end of each binding strip.

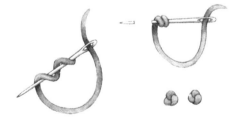

To work a French knot, bring the thread out at the required position and hold it down to one side with the left thumb. Twist the thread twice around the needle, then insert it back into the fabric close to the starting point. Pull the thread through to the back, tightening the knot. Bring the needle up again for next knot.

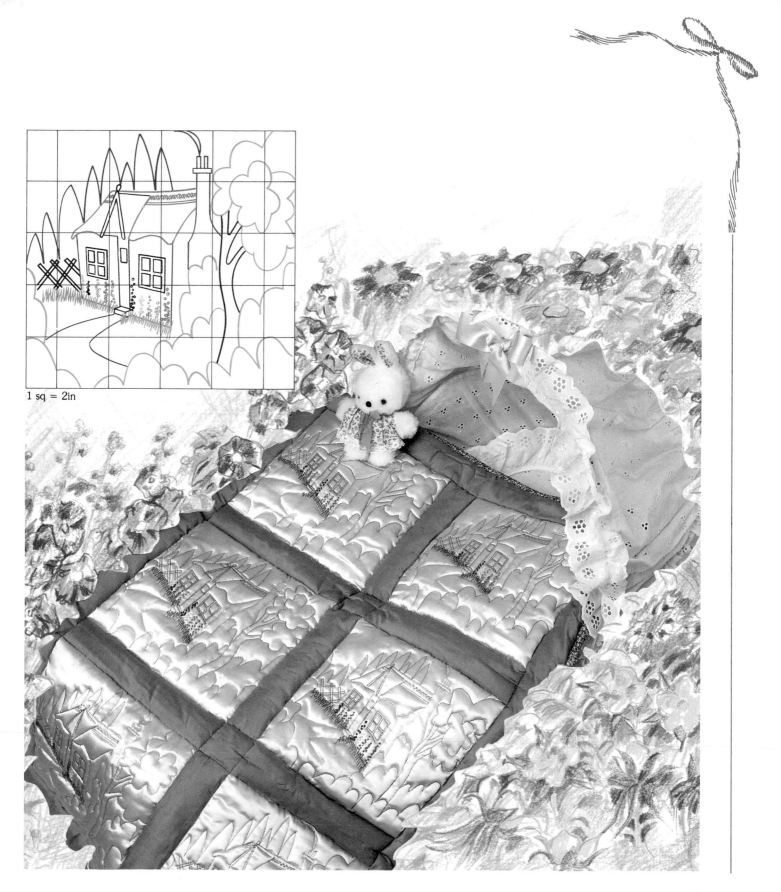

1 sq = 2in

STORY QUILT

Any baby grows to love a quilt like this with nursery tale characters and motifs appliquéd onto it.

The design for this crib quilt has been taken from the story of Goldilocks and the three bears, but any fairytale or nursery rhyme could provide characters and motifs for an interesting quilt. From an illustrated book, you could easily trace the motifs, divide each picture into squares and enlarge it as required, using dressmaker's graph paper.

All materials should be pre-shrunk and colorfast. Try to choose an appropriate fabric for each motif. Use small prints in green for tree foliage, brown for tree trunks, gingham for the tablecloth and floral prints for the flower borders. Use small prints or stripes for clothes and eyelet for the apron.

⅝in seam allowances are included throughout unless otherwise specified.

Cutting out
Cut out two pieces of poplin, each measuring 44½in by 30¾in. Cut two pieces of batting to the same size. Cut out four 5½in wide border strips, two 44½in long and two 30¾in long.

Preparing the appliqué motifs
Using dressmaker's graph paper, enlarge all appliqué motifs on the graph pattern on pages 48-9 to the correct size and carefully cut out the pattern pieces.

Back the fabrics you have selected for the appliqué design with fusible interfacing.

Using the pattern pieces, cut out the motifs from appropriate fabrics. Also cut out several pieces from floral fabric.

Using a fine brush and diluting the paint as required, paint the face and hands of Goldilocks and the faces and paws of the three bears. Use the blue fabric paint for Goldilocks's eyes, the red paint for her mouth and the black paint for her hands and the bears' faces and paws.

You will need
For a quilt measuring 29½in × 43½in
1¾yd of 45in-wide cream poplin
¾yd of 45in-wide printed cotton for the border
Assorted printed cotton for appliqué motifs
Thread
One small pot each of black, red and blue fabric paint
Fusible interfacing
2⅝yd of 36in-wide medium-weight batting
Dressmaker's graph paper
Fine paintbrush

With this quilt, the border strips are hemmed along the long edges and pinned in place on the main piece (right). The appliqué motifs, backed with interfacing, are then positioned and zig-zag stitched around the edges (far right), after which the edges of the border strips are also zig-zagged.

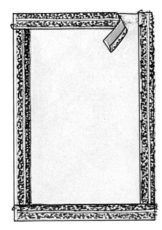

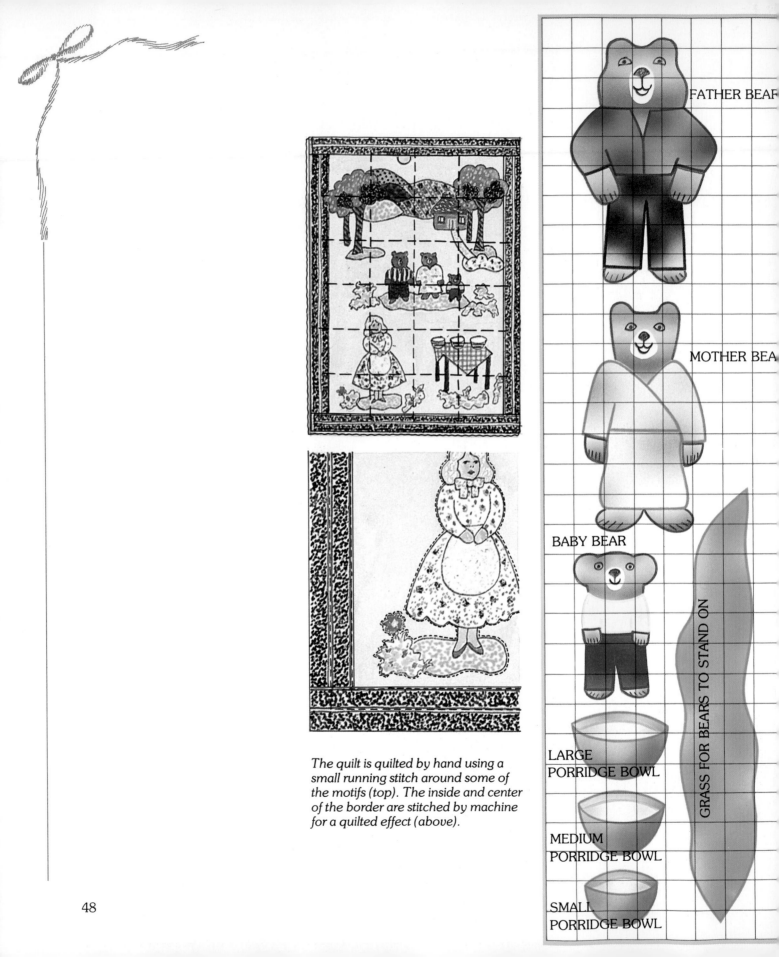

The quilt is quilted by hand using a small running stitch around some of the motifs (top). The inside and center of the border are stitched by machine for a quilted effect (above).

FATHER BEAR

MOTHER BEAR

BABY BEAR

GRASS FOR BEARS TO STAND ON

LARGE PORRIDGE BOWL

MEDIUM PORRIDGE BOWL

SMALL PORRIDGE BOWL

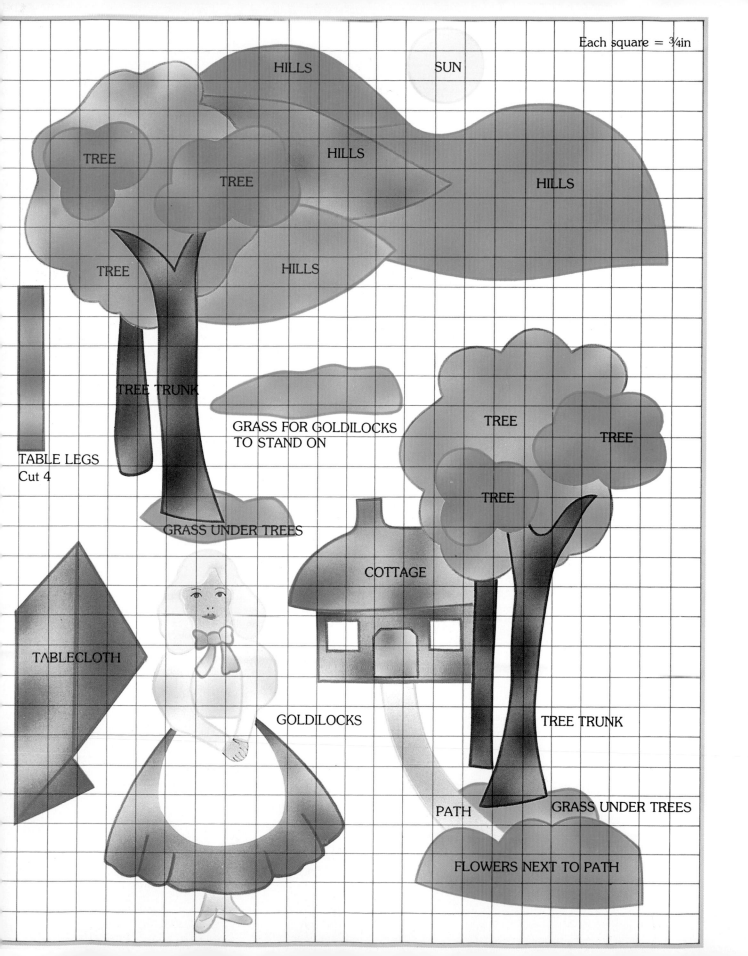

Each square = ¾in

HILLS

SUN

TREE

HILLS

TREE

HILLS

HILLS

TREE

HILLS

TREE TRUNK

GRASS FOR GOLDILOCKS
TO STAND ON

TABLE LEGS
Cut 4

TREE

TREE

TREE

GRASS UNDER TREES

COTTAGE

TABLECLOTH

GOLDILOCKS

TREE TRUNK

PATH

GRASS UNDER TREES

FLOWERS NEXT TO PATH

Making the border

Turn under ⅜in on one long edge of each strip and place the long strips along the long edges of one poplin piece, raw edges matching; pin in place. Turn under the edges of the short strips and position along the short edges in the same way.

Arranging the appliqué

Place all appliqué motifs on the right side of the poplin and move them around until the right balance is achieved. If any pieces overlap the border, tuck them underneath the borders, except the trees, which should overlap the border. Pin and baste in place. With a fairly wide, close zig-zag, stitch all the motifs in place, using matching thread. Stitch the border in place all around the inside edge.

Quilting the picture

Lay the picture, right side up, on a piece of batting. Baste all the layers together vertically and horizontally, starting from the center and working outward. Quilt by hand with a small running stitch around some of the images.

Joining back and front

Place the remaining pieces of batting and poplin together and baste together as before.
Place the front and back together, poplin sides together and raw edges matching. Pin, baste and stitch ⅝in from the edge all around, leaving a 12in gap along one short edge. Turn right side out and slip stitch the opening to close.
Stitch by machine along the inside and the center of the border to give a more quilted effect.

Part of the fun of making this quilt is choosing appropriate prints for the characters and motifs. Shown below are suitable alternatives to the fabrics used in the photograph on page 47. The three swatches on the left could be used for tree foliage, the brown print for tree trunks, the yellow check for the tablecloth, the yellow and green flower print for flower borders and the four swatches on the right for clothing.

RIBBON QUILT

The colors, pattern and silky softness of this ribbon appliquéd crib quilt will appeal to babies and parents alike.

This is the simplest method of appliqué yet gives very dramatic results. Satin ribbon is fused to transfer fusing web, which has been fused to fabric, and the ribbon is then stitched. Because ribbon appliqué is difficult to do over large areas of fabric, the quilt is made from small panels. The quilting is done after the panels are sewn together, and the quilt is then trimmed with a ribbon border. The baby's initials are embroidered onto the quilt using satin stitch.
⅝in seam allowances are included throughout unless otherwise specified.

Cutting out
Following the quilt plan on page 53, make a paper pattern. Cut along dotted lines to divide pattern into pieces for quilt top. Pin to fabric and cut out, leaving ⅝in seam allowances. Draw lines to indicate the direction in which ribbons should be placed.

Applying the ribbons
Cut a piece of transfer fusing web to fit each area of fabric to be covered by ribbons, except the border. The border is stitched in place once the panels are joined. Following manufacturer's instructions, fuse the web to the fabric. Now peel back the paper to expose the adhesive web and, beginning at the center of the fabric, place the first few ribbons in position on top of the web, using the quilt plan as a guide. Fold paper back over ribbons and press to fuse ribbons to web. Continue until all ribbons are in place. Cut ends of ribbon to the exact required length.
Using either matching or contrasting thread, stitch along each side of each length of ribbon. Work all stitching in any one color before rethreading the machine. (If your machine has a twin-needle attachment, you can speed up the sewing of ribbons by stitching along the two edges of adjoining ribbons at once.)

Embroidering the initials
Trace the letters of your choice from the alphabet on the pattern on pages 54-7. Using dressmaker's carbon and tracing wheel, transfer letters to plain satin triangle.
Place the initialled fabric in an 8in embroidery hoop and, using two strands of embroidery thread, satin stitch initials onto the fabric, following the instructions given on the right.

Assembling the quilt
Arrange the seven center panels so ribbons form zig zags (see quilt plan on page 53). Match ends of ribbons and right sides together, raw edges even, sew the seven center panels together.
Working in the same way, sew the three sections for the remaining two corners of the quilt together. Sew to the center panel.

You will need
For a crib quilt measuring approximately 41½in × 29½in
About 68yd of single-faced satin ribbon in ⅛in, ¼in and ⅜in widths in about 14 different colors
9yd of ⅞in-wide single-faced satin ribbon for the border
1⅝yd of 45in-wide cream cotton fabric
15in by 15in piece of washable cream satin fabric
1⅝yd of medium-weight batting
2¼yd of 15in-wide transfer fusing web
Stranded embroidery thread
Thread

To embroider satin stitch, bring the needle up on one edge of the area to be embroidered, carry the thread across to the opposite edge and return under the fabric to the starting point. Work the next stitch close to the first, making sure no background fabric shows in between. For large shapes, work several short stitches across the area rather than one long stitch.

Place batting on the underside of the quilt top, baste in position and trim even with all edges. Using a wide zig-zag stitch and working from the center outward, quilt seams of zig-zag panels. Then, quilt seams of other two corners.

Cut border ribbon into two 4½yd pieces. Wrong sides together, sew

The quilt plan (left above) shows the arrangement of the ribbons on each of the individual fabric panels. After the ribbons are appliquéd to the fabric, the panels are stitched together. The baby's initials are embroidered on satin (left below) using the alphabets on pages 54-7 as a pattern, and the satin piece is then sewn to the quilt.

along one long edge. Leaving 1in free at each end, topstitch one free edge of ribbon to right side of quilt along each edge.

Baste the second layer of batting and backing to quilt top. Trim edges level with top. Fold ribbon to the back of quilt and hand sew to backing. Fold ribbon under to form a miter at each corner and stitch.

54

UVW

abcdefgh

pqrstu

XYZ

ijklmno

vwxyz

BABY'S DAY

In this chapter you'll find the extras that make caring for a baby so much easier. There is a whole range of accessories for taking a baby on trips away from home. Two styles of changing bags are included, one with zipped sides (page 101) and the other with pockets (page 104).

You can make a wide variety of items for carrying a baby. The sturdy fabric carry cot (page 74) and the lined baby basket (page 71) make cozy portable beds where a baby can sleep soundly. Many babies like the reassurance of being close to a parent, and the two baby slings (pages 82 and 86), which are worn at the front, leave the parent's hands free. The back baby carrier (page 79) is another style, which gives the baby a good view. For a traditional baby carriage, there is an exquisite patchwork quilt on page 60.

Other accessories are designed for use around the home. A bouncing chair is ideal for a young baby, and you can easily give an old bouncing chair a bright new cover, either quilted (page 90) or appliquéd (page 95). For more bouncing, with an older baby, sew a bouncing swing by reviving an old one with a new seat, as shown on page 98. On page 64 there's an unusual crocheted quilt that is perfect for use as a play rug on the floor. Finally, the towel set with appliquéd teddybears on page 108 will make a perfect end to a baby's day.

This charming carriage quilt, featuring cathedral window patchwork, will make a very pretty heirloom.

"Cathedral window" is a traditional patchwork design, in which foundation squares are folded and refolded then sewn together and decorated with brightly colored patches. The resulting effect of intricate tracery surrounding vividly colored panels gives the technique its name. ¼in seam allowances are included on the patchwork and the ruffle, and ⅜in seam allowances are included on the quilt edges.

You will need
For a quilt measuring approximately 27½in by 22in

1⅛yd of 36in-wide white cotton lawn
⅝yd of 45in-wide red on white floral cotton print
⅝yd of 45in-wide blue on white floral cotton print
⅞yd of 45in-wide blue floral cotton print
½yd of 45in-wide contrasting white and blue floral cotton print
3yd of ⅜in-wide red velvet ribbon
⅞yd of 45in-wide medium-weight polyester batting
Thread
Graph paper
Thin cardboard for patterns

Cutting out the squares
Make a square pattern. Draw and cut out a 6¼in square from graph paper. Using this as a guide, cut out your pattern from thin cardboard. From white cotton lawn, using the pattern, cut out twenty-four squares. Align the sides of the pattern with the straight grain of the fabric.
Make a second pattern, 1¾in square, in the same way. Using the 1¾in pattern, cut out a selection of squares from the red on white and blue on white floral print cotton fabrics.

Preparing the white squares
On one white square turn all the edges under ¼in. Fold in each corner of the square to meet in the center. Pin to hold. The square now measures 4⅛in.
Fold each corner of this square in toward the center. Pin to hold, removing the previous pins. Fasten the corners together at the center with a few neat stitches to hold them. The square now measures 3in. It is important to maintain accuracy at this stage to achieve good results. Fold all the white squares in the same way.
Begin sewing the squares together: position four white squares together,

Cathedral window patchwork involves folding foundation squares. After the edges are turned in, the four corners are folded to meet in the center (right above). Each corner of the new square is then folded in and fastened with a few stitches (far right above). The squares are sewn together with whipstitches (right below), and colored patches are basted in position over the sewn together white squares, covering the stitches. Finally, adjoining folded edges of the white squares are rolled and turned over the raw edges of the colored squares and sewn in place, forming a slight curve (far right below).

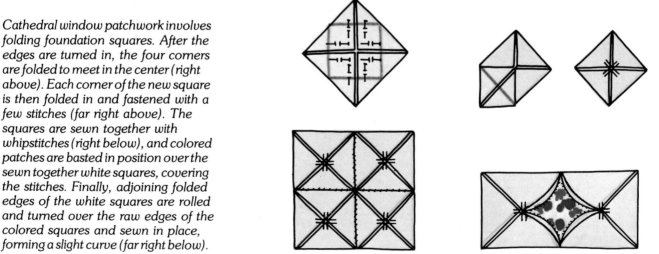

matching sides. Sew the squares together on their adjoining sides with small whipstitches. Repeat until the 24 squares have been joined together to form a rectangle six squares long and four squares wide.

Positioning the floral squares

Work out a pleasing pattern with the red on white and blue on white floral cotton print squares. Position the floral squares in the center of the stitched together squares, over the whipstitches. Pin in place. Move the

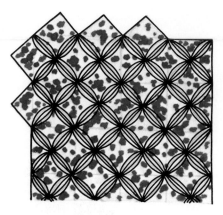

At the side edges of the patchwork, only two sides are rolled over. The remaining halves of the squares are turned under, to make a straight edge.

floral squares around until a good design is formed. Baste the floral squares in position. At the side edges, only half of the floral squares will be attached.

Completing the patchwork

Begin at one floral square: roll and turn an adjoining folded edge of the white fabric over the raw edge of the floral square. It will form a gentle curve. Taking small stitches, sew the white fabric in position, right through all the fabric thicknesses. Work around all four sides of the floral square.

Repeat with all floral squares of fabric. At the side edges, roll over the two sides only. Fold the remaining half of each square to the wrong side; pin and baste in place.

When the patchwork is completed, press the work gently on the wrong side with a steam iron or over a damp cloth.

Attaching the blue floral background

From blue floral print fabric cut out two pieces each 22¾in by 17¼in for background. Align the sides of each piece with the straight grain of the fabric.

Place one blue floral print fabric piece with right side up. Position the wrong side of the patchwork fabric in the center of the right side of the blue fabric piece. Pin, baste and neatly sew the patchwork fabric in place around all side edges.

Adding the ribbon trim

Cut the velvet ribbon into four lengths: two 28¼in long and two 22¾in long.

Starting at one corner of patchwork center: leave about 5½in of ribbon free at each side, pin and baste one short length of ribbon along short edge of patchwork center over previous stitches. Hand sew both sides of the ribbon in place. Repeat at opposite short edge of patchwork fabric. Then repeat with the long lengths of ribbon at each long side of the patchwork center. Tie the excess ribbon at each corner into a neat bow. Hand sew the bows neatly in place.

Making the ruffle

For the ruffle, from the contrasting white and blue floral cotton print cut out four strips 3½in wide from across the width of the fabric.

Position two ruffle pieces with wrong sides together, matching edges. Pin, baste and stitch a ¼in seam along one short edge. Refold, with right sides together and stitch just over ¼in from folded edge, to form a French seam. Repeat, stitching all the ruffle pieces together in the same way, forming a ring shape.

Turn under a double ¼in hem along one long edge of the ruffle piece. Pin, baste and topstitch hem. Sew two rows of gathering stitches along the raw edge of the ruffle piece.

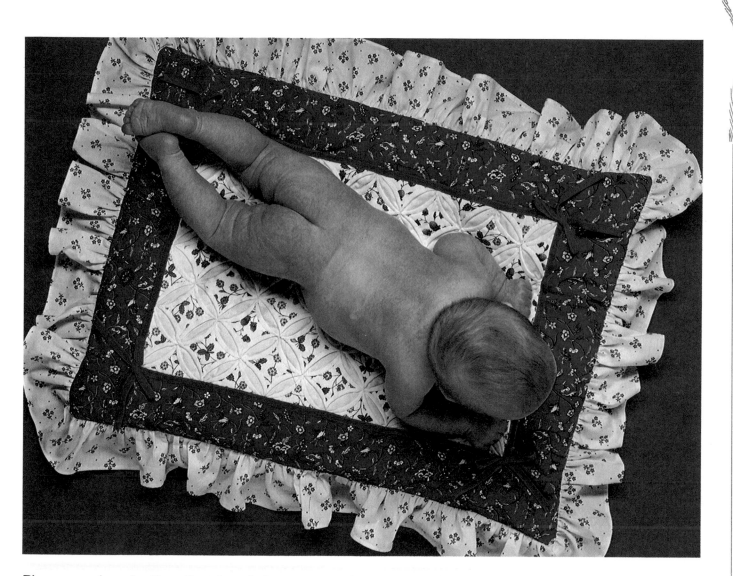

Place raw edge of ruffle with right side facing outer edge of patchworked piece. Pull up the gathering stitches on the ruffle evenly to fit. Pin, baste and stitch with a ⅜in seam.

Assembling the quilt

Position second blue floral cotton print piece with right side to patchwork piece, over ruffle. Pin, baste and stitch all around following previous stitching line, and leaving an 8in opening in one short side. Trim seam allowance and cut across corners. Turn quilt right side out.

From batting cut out two pieces each 22in by 16½in. Place batting pieces together with all edges matching. Insert double batting into quilt, pushing well into the corners. Turn under opening edges. Slip stitch folded edges neatly together to close.

CROCHETED QUILT

This quilt is great for taking along on trips so a baby will have a comfortable companion to play on or to snuggle under.

A list of the abbreviations used is given on page 5.

You will need
For a quilt measuring 35in long by 25¾in wide
Sport yarn:
13oz in main color A (green)
6oz in each of 2 contrasting colors B (red) and C (white)
Sizes E and F crochet hooks
3½yd of 36in-wide synthetic padding
Thread to match B

Gauge
One motif measures 5½in by 4¾in

Each square of the quilt is worked separately and joined later. Single crochet is used throughout. A washable padding is placed between the front and the back and the two pieces are joined along the sides. Lines are stitched along the motif seams to form the quilting. Last, the quilt is edged with a picot border.
A list of the abbreviations used is given on page 5.
The stitch used throughout is single crochet. When changing colors in the middle of a row it must be remembered that the color is changed on the last yo of the last stitch worked before the stitch in the new color as foll: using first color insert hook in next st and draw yarn through, as if to make a sc, drop the color being used, yarn over hook with 2nd color and draw through 2nd color, so 2nd color is ready to be used for next st.

Plain motif for back (make 30)
Using larger hook and A, ch24.
Base row 1sc in 2nd ch from hook, 1sc in each ch to end. Turn. 23sc.
Pat row Ch1, 1sc in each sc to end. Turn.
Rep pat row 27 times. Fasten off.

Motif 1 (make 12)
Using larger hook and B, ch25.
1st row Working first st in 2nd ch from hook and 1sc in each ch work 2 A, 2 C, 16 B, 2 C, 2 A. Turn. 24sc.
2nd row Ch1, 3 A, 2 C, 14 B, 2 C, 3 A. Turn.
3rd row Ch1, 1 C, 3 A, 2 C, 12 B, 2 C, 3 A, 1 C. Turn.
4th row Ch1, 2 C, 3 A, 2 C, 10 B, 2 C, 3 A, 2 C. Turn.
5th row Ch1, 1 B, 2 C, 3 A, 2 C, 8 B, 2 C, 3 A, 2 C, 1 B. Turn.
6th row Ch1, 2 B, 2 C, 3 A, 2 C, 6 B, 2 C, 3 A, 2 C, 2 B. Turn.
7th row Ch1, 3 B, 2 C, 3 A, 2 C, 4 B, 2 C, 3 A, 2 C, 3 B. Turn.
8th row Ch1, 4 B, 2 C, 3 A, 2 C, 2 B, 2 C, 3 A, 2 C, 4 B. Turn.
9th row Ch1, 5 B, 2 C, 3 A, 1 C, 2 B, 1 C, 3 A, 2 C, 5 B. Turn.
10th row Ch1, 6 B, 2 C, 3 A, 2 C, 3 A, 2 C, 6 B. Turn.
11th row Ch1, 7 B, 2 C, 6 A, 2 C, 7 B. Turn.
12th row Ch1, 9 B, 1 C, 4 A, 1 C, 9 B. Turn.
13th – 24th rows Work 12th – first rows in this order.
Fasten off.

Motif 2 (make 6)
Using larger hook and C, ch25.
1st row Working first st in 2nd ch from hook and 1sc in each ch work (4 C, 4 B) 3 times. Turn. 24sc.
2nd row Ch1, (4 B, 4 C) 3 times. Turn
3rd row Ch1, (4 C, 4 B) 3 times. Turn.
4th row Ch1, (4 B, 4 C) 3 times. Turn.

5th row Ch1, (4 C, 4 B) 3 times. Turn.
6th row Ch1, (4 B, 4 C) 3 times. Turn.
Rep these 6 rows 3 times more. Fasten off.

Motif 3 (make 6)
Using larger hook and B, ch25.
1st row Using B, 1sc in 2nd ch from hook, 1sc in each ch to end.
Turn. 24sc.

1	2	3	4	1
1	4	2	3	1
1	3	4	2	1
1	2	3	4	1
1	4	2	3	1
1	3	4	2	1

Motif key

2nd and 3rd rows Using B, ch1, 1sc in each sc to end. Turn.
4th row Ch1, 3 C, (2 B, 2 C) 4 times, 2 B, 3 C. Turn.
5th row As 4th row.
6th row Using C, as 2nd row. Turn.
7th – 12th rows Rep 2nd – 6th rows, using A in place of B.
Rep last 12 rows once more. Fasten off.

Motif 4 (make 6)
Using larger hook and A, ch25.
1st row Using A, 1sc in 2nd ch from hook, 1sc in each ch to end. Turn.
24sc.
2nd row Using A, 1sc in each sc to end. Turn.
3rd row Ch1, 5 A, 2 B, 4 A, 2 C, 4 A, 2 B, 5 A. Turn.
4th row Ch1, 4 A, 4 B, 2 A, 4 C, 2 A, 4 B, 4 A. Turn.
5th row As 4th row.
6th row As 3rd row.
7th row Ch1, 2 A, 2 C, 4 A, 2 B, 4 A, 2 B, 4 A, 2 C, 2 A. Turn.
8th row Ch1, 1 A, 4 C, 2 A, 4 B, 2 A, 4 B, 2 A, 4 C, 1 A. Turn.
9th row As 8th row.
10th row As 7th row.
11th row Ch1, 5 A, 2 C, (4 A, 2 C) twice, 5 A. Turn.
12th row Ch1, 4 A, 4 C, 2 A, 4 B, 2 A, 4 C, 4 A. Turn.
13th row As 12th row.
14th row As 11th row.
15th – 22nd rows As 7th – 14th rows.
23rd and 24th rows As 2nd row.
Fasten off.

To finish
Weave in all loose ends. Join all the plain motifs into a rectangle of 5 motifs by 6 motifs to form back. Join the colored motifs foll the motif key on this page for position. Fold the padding into 3 equal layers, lay the top section of cover on top of the padding and pin all around. Cut the padding slightly smaller than the cover. Then, using matching thread, machine stitch on the right side of work across line of joins. Place the plain back of the cover with right side out onto the padding.
With colored motifs up, using smaller hook and A, and working through both the front and back sections, work 1sc in each sc on short edges, 1sc in each row end on side edges, and 3sc in each corner all around edge, join with a sl st to first sc. Turn.
Next round Ch1, 1sc in each sc and 3sc in the center sc at each corner, join with a sl st to first sc. Turn.
Rep last round twice more.
Picot round Ch1, *1sc in each of next 3sc, ch3, sl st in last sc made, rep from * all around, join with a sl st to first sc.
Fasten off.
Press edging lightly, foll instructions on yarn label.

IP-UP SLEEPER

**Make bedtime a delight with a cuddly sleeper featuring a
colorful smiling clown or other fun motif.**

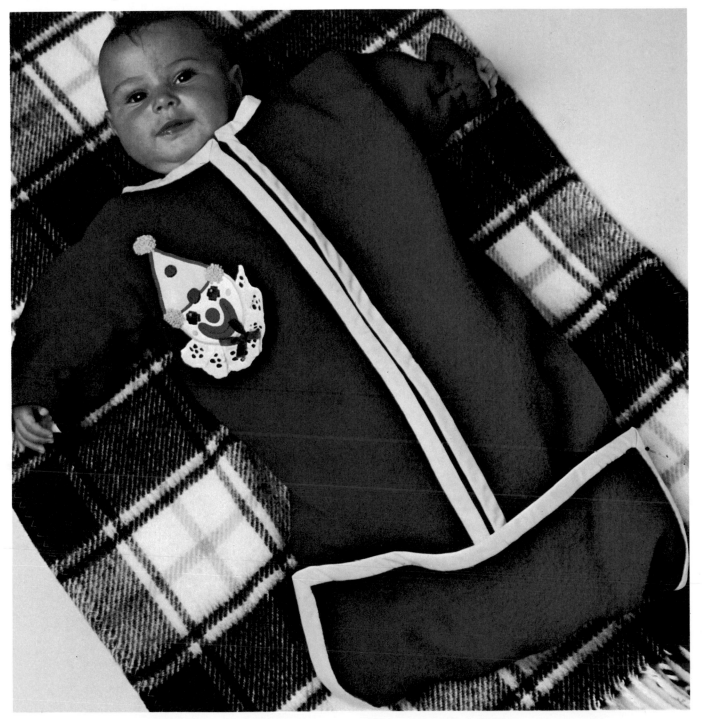

You will need

For a sleeper with a finished length of 21¾in, to fit age 9 months and older
⅞yd of 48/54in-wide or 1¼yd of 36in-wide synthetic fur fabric, fleece or ready-quilted cotton
1¼yd of 36in-wide lining fabric
⅝yd of 36in-wide fabric for binding
Thread
⅝yd of elastic
22in open-ended zipper
Eight snaps
Appliqué motif or scraps of fabric to use for appliqué

This zipper-fronted sleeper, made from a cozy fabric like synthetic fur or fleece, will keep a baby warm and snug at night. It is especially useful for those babies who tend to kick off their blankets in their sleep. When the baby grows older, the sleeper can easily be adapted to make a bathrobe by removing the snaps, cutting off the bottom flap and binding the back edge to match the front.

⅝in seam allowances are included throughout unless otherwise specified.

Cutting out

Place the fabric on table or cutting board, right side down. Mark one back section, two fronts and two sleeves, following the measurement diagram and cutting layout below. If using synthetic fur, arrange all the pieces so that the pile runs in the same direction down the length of the garment; cut only one thickness of fabric at a time. On the back section, mark the foldline with a line of basting. Cut out the lining, and cut bias strips for binding to make a total length of 110in.

Making the motif

Trace the pieces for the clown's head from the photograph, or trace one

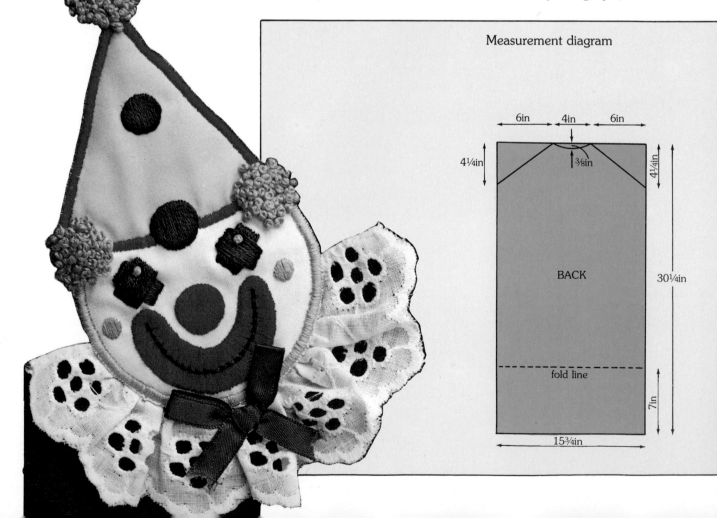

Measurement diagram

6in   4in   6in

4¼in   ⅜in   4¼in

BACK

30¼in

fold line

7in

15¾in

of the motifs on page 70. Cut out pieces from scraps of fabric in appropriate colors. Pin and baste the pieces to the right front of the sleeper, centering them on the section and positioning them about 6in from the top. Set the stitch length with a very short zig-zag and stitch in place over the raw edges, or by hand using blanket stitch (see page 70). If making the clown, use eyelet for the ruffle; sew the hair and pompom with tight French knots (see page 44) and use satin stitch (see page 51) for the features, adding a ribbon bow.

Making the sleeper

With right sides together, raw edges even, pin, baste and stitch sleeves to back and fronts at shoulder seams. If using synthetic fur, stitch with a small zig-zag stitch; after stitching, shave the pile from the seam allowances, or trim with small scissors; then, on the right side, pull out the pile that has been caught in the seam, using a pin. If using ready-quilted fabric, trim away the batting within the seam allowance. Press seams open.

Fold sleeper in half along shoulders, right sides together, matching underarm and side seams. Pin, baste and stitch seams from cuff to

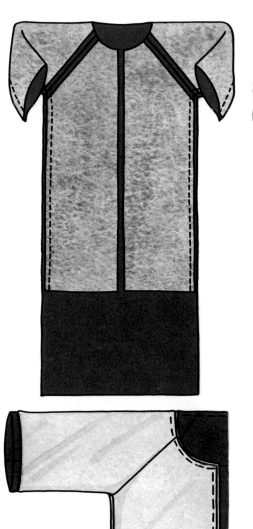

The sleeper is made by first stitching the sleeves to the back and fronts at the shoulder seams then stitching from cuff to hem in one seam at each side (top). A lining is made in the same way and basted to the sleeper around the neckline and down the front, then the wrists are finished with an elastic casing (above). Finally, the edges are bound, a zipper is put in down the front and snaps are sewn on for the flap at the bottom.

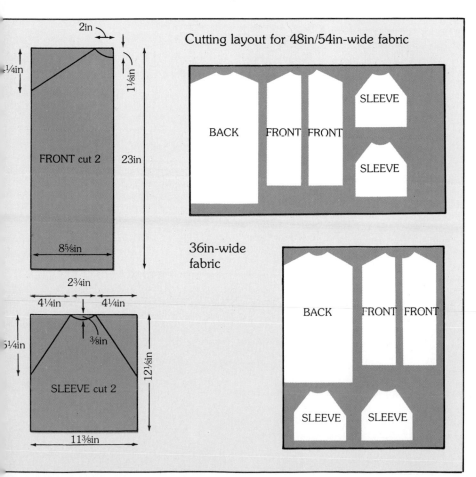

69

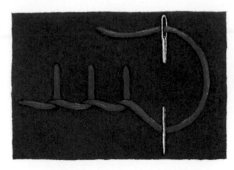

To embroider blanket stitch, working from left to right, bring the needle out on the stitch line. Hold the thread to the right and make a downward vertical stitch bringing the needle out over the thread. Repeat, inserting the needle a short distance away, depending on the stitch size.

underarm and then to hem as far as line of basting on back. Press seams open.

Lining the sleeper

Cut out and make up lining in the same way and turn right side out. Slip completed lining over the (inside-out) sleeper, wrong sides together and seams matching. Pin and baste together around neck and down front edges, keeping raw edges together.

At wrist edge, turn under ⅝in of outer fabric and ¾in of lining. Slip stitch together around cuff. Sew two lines of stitches around cuff, ¾in and 1⅛in from finished edge, to form a casing for the elastic. Make a hole in the seam of the lining and thread elastic through. Cut elastic to fit wrist, allowing ¾in for sewing together. Stitch ends securely.

Stitch prepared binding all around neck, fronts, front hem and back flap, mitering corners. Insert an open-ended zipper in the front opening. Sew six snaps across the lower edge of the bottom flap, on the lined side of the flap. Sew two more on the sides of the flap. Sew opposite halves of snaps to front sections to match. If using synthetic fur or fleece, press fabric on the wrong side, using a velvet board or towel to prevent flattening.

Either of these motifs may be used instead of the clown. Appliqué the pieces in the same way, using machine zig-zagging for the balloon strings.

LINED BABY BASKET & QUILT

Give a plain basket a cheerful quilted lining with a matching quilt, for a small baby to sleep in when traveling.

For ease of quilting, choose a geometric print like checked gingham for the lining fabric. Keep the lining in place inside the basket with neat ties. ⅜in seam allowances are included throughout unless otherwise specified.

Cutting out

For the lining, measure the base length and width on the outside of the basket at the widest points; these will be the dimensions of the base piece. For the side pieces of the lining, mark the center of both long sides, then measure around the edge of the basket from one mark to the opposite mark, then from that mark back to the first mark. Add ¾in to each measurement; these will be the lengths of the two side pieces. Measure from base to top at the highest point, and add ¾in; this will be the depth of the side pieces. Cut out rectangles for one base piece and

You will need
Cotton fabric
Medium-weight batting
Muslin (or plain cotton or an old sheet)
1in-wide bias binding
1⅛in-wide ruffled eyelet edging
Thread

71

two side pieces from the cotton and again from the muslin and the batting. The pieces will be shaped to the basket after quilting.
For the binding and edging, measure around the top edge of the basket and add ¾in for a seam allowance and 30in for each of the four ties.
For the quilt, cut out two pieces from cotton and one from batting the width of the basket plus allowance for tucking in, and the desired length.

Making the base and side pieces

For base, place cotton and muslin together, sandwiching batting in between. Pin and baste together, then quilt. (If you are using gingham, quilt the fabric squares both ways across four of the woven squares.) Repeat for the two side pieces.
Place the quilted base fabric on a flat surface. Place basket in the center on muslin side of the fabric. Mark around the base of the basket, using dressmaker's chalk.
Finish the side edges of both side pieces with zig-zag stitching, catching in the raw edges of each of the three fabrics with a medium-size stitch.

Place side pieces right sides together, matching raw edges. Stitch each side seam with a ⅜in seam, to make up the complete side piece.

Run a line of gathering stitches around the base edge of the side piece, stitching between the seams using a large machine stitch, or gathering the fabric by hand. Mark the center of long side edges of base. Pull up gathers evenly and match up the marks with the seams on the base edge of the side piece. Pin side to base. Baste and stitch the side piece to the base, with a ⅜in seam. Before stitching, check that the gathers are evenly spaced around the base.

To finish base seam of cover, zig-zag stitch around the raw edges using a medium stitch. Make sure all the fabrics are caught up as you stitch.

Finishing the top edge

Place lining inside basket, with wrong side against wicker. Match seams on sides to center of basket sides. Mark along top edge of side level with basket top, holding the lining inside the basket with small pieces of double-sided cellophane tape.

Unfold one edge of bias binding. Place unfolded edge along right-side top edge of side, beginning and ending at one of the side seams. Stitch binding to fabric through creased line. Join bias binding together at side seam on the straight of grain with a plain flat seam. Fold binding over the raw edge to the wrong side. Pin, baste and slip stitch folded edge of binding in place over previous stitching line, along top edge.

Pin eyelet around top edge of lining, placing the edge against the edge of the bias binding, and beginning and ending at one of the side seams. Join eyelet together to fit at side seam with a plain flat seam. Zig-zag in place.

Making the ties

Cut four ties from bias binding. Turn under ⅜in at raw ends of each tie, then fold ties in half lengthwise. Stitch edges together.

Place lining inside basket, matching seams of cover to center of basket. Mark the positions of the handles to show the position of the binding ties. Remove lining from basket. Fold one tie in half and place center on wrong side of lining over marked position on bound edge. Repeat for each tie. Stitch ties in place with two rows of stitching and finish with a few backstitches.

Place completed lining inside basket, matching ties to handles. Thread a tie through base of handle and tie into a bow. Repeat with remaining ties.

Making the quilt

From cotton and batting, cut out quilt pieces. Place cotton pieces together sandwiching batting. Quilt the fabric. Curve base edges following basket edges, folding the quilt in half lengthwise before rounding the corners to make them the same shape.

Bind short raw edges of quilt and add edging, as for the top edge of the lining. Bind all remaining edges, turning under raw edges of binding at top edge to finish.

CARRY COT

Made like a sleeping bag, but with a sturdy base and handles, this solves the problem of carrying around a sleepy baby.

The fiberboard base of the carry cot gives stability as well as some protection from the surface upon which it rests. A piece of foam counteracts the hardness of the fiberboard. The carry cot is fastened with heavyweight zippers, stitched in place with zipper guards to prevent the baby's clothing or bedding from being caught in the teeth of the zipper. The best fabric for the carry cot is cotton or a cotton mixture, which is hardwearing, washable and colorfast. Choose a color that will not look grubby after a few trips.

⅝in seam allowances are included throughout unless otherwise specified.

Preparing the base
Round off the corners of the fiberboard: at both short ends mark two points 4¾in in from the corners. In the same way, mark 4¾in down each side. Using a plate or saucer, draw a curved line to join the two points around each corner. Using a coping saw, cut away the corners along the curved lines. Smooth the cut corners with sandpaper.

Using the fiberboard as a pattern, cut out the foam: place the fiberboard on the foam, matching the straight edges. Using a felt tipped pen, mark the rounded corners on the foam. Using a large pair of dressmaking scissors, cut around the corners along the marked lines.

Cutting out
Using the fiberboard as a pattern, cut out the following pieces: two pieces of contrasting fabric for the mattress cover, 1¼in larger than the fiberboard at the sides and top edge, and 4in longer at the bottom. Cut out one piece of main fabric and one piece of contrasting fabric, 1¼in larger all around for the base and base lining. Cut out one piece of main fabric 10in shorter than the fiberboard at the top edge for the top cover, cutting the top edge straight, and one piece of contrasting fabric 3½in shorter than the fiberboard at the top edge for the lining cover, again cutting the top edge straight across.

For the sides, make a paper pattern: measure the distance around the fiberboard base from center top to center bottom and add 1¼in for the seam allowances, then cut a piece of paper this long and 8in wide. Shape the pattern as shown in the diagram on page 77, graduating the sides from the top end down to 5in at the bottom end. Check that this piece will fit around the base.

Using this pattern, cut out two pieces of main fabric and two pieces of contrasting fabric for lining.

For the handles cut out two strips of main fabric, each 43½in by 6in.

From the batting, using fabric pieces as patterns, cut out one base, one top cover 21¾in long, two side pieces and two handle strips. From the interfacing, using the pattern for the sides, cut out two pieces that will fit around the head section.

You will need
2¼yd of 48in-wide furnishing cotton/polyester fabric

2⅝yd of 48in-wide furnishing cotton/polyester in a contrasting color

Two 18in-long zippers

2⅝yd of 36in-wide medium-weight batting

20in by 12in piece of heavyweight interfacing

30in by 12in piece of fiberboard, ⅛in thick

30in by 12in piece of foam, ⅜in thick

Thread

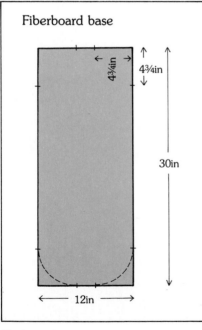

Fiberboard base

4¾in

4¾in

30in

12in

To form the carry cot base, a fiberboard rectangle is rounded off at the corners. This base is used as a pattern for the foam and fabric.

Making the mattress cover

Place the mattress cover pieces with right sides together, matching all edges. Pin, baste and stitch together with a ⅝in seam, leaving the bottom edge open. Make a narrow double hem along each bottom edge; pin, baste and topstitch hems in place.

Place the foam on one side of fiberboard, matching all edges. Slip the mattress cover over both fiberboard and the foam, tucking in the excess at the base to hold the foam in place.

Making the outer cover

Pin and baste the batting side pieces to the wrong side of the main fabric side pieces. Quilt both side pieces, with the fabric motifs being positioned in the center of each quilted square if possible.

Place the two quilted side pieces with right sides together. Pin, baste and stitch the short seams at the top and bottom with a ⅝in seam. Press open.

Quilt the base in the same way as side pieces. With right sides together and raw edges even, stitch the lower edge of the side piece to the edge of the base with a ⅝in seam, matching top and bottom seams of side piece to center top and center bottom of base.

Making the handles

Pin and baste batting to wrong side of each handle strip. Quilt the fabric as with side pieces. With right sides together, pin, baste and stitch the two handle strips together along two short sides. With right sides together, fold handle piece in half lengthwise; pin, baste and stitch all around with a ⅝in seam and leaving an 8in-wide opening along the long edge. Trim seam allowances and clip corners. Turn handle piece right side out. Turn in opening edges and slip stitch together to close.

Place handle piece across base about 7½in from top and about 8½in from the bottom edge. Match short seams to center of base; pin and baste in place. Check this positioning so that the baby's head will be slightly raised when the carry cot is being carried. Stitch each handle firmly to base with a rectangle of stitching on each side of the short seam. Stitch each handle to the side pieces with two shorter rectangles.

Making the top cover

With right sides together, pin, baste and stitch short straight edge of top cover to lining. Pin and baste batting to wrong side of top cover, so that there is a 3in-wide band of contrasting fabric at the top. Quilt the top cover as before.

The pattern for the sides is made by measuring around the fiberboard from the center of one end to the center of the other end. This gives the length of one side piece. The other dimensions are as shown in the diagram below, with the height at the top end graduating down as shown. The two side pieces are quilted, sewn together at both ends then sewn to the quilted base (bottom left). The handle strips are quilted then sewn together to form one handle piece. After being folded in half lengthwise, stitched together and turned right side out, the handle piece is sewn securely to the carry cot base and sides (bottom right), forming two very strong handles.

21½in

8in

Pattern for side pieces

5in

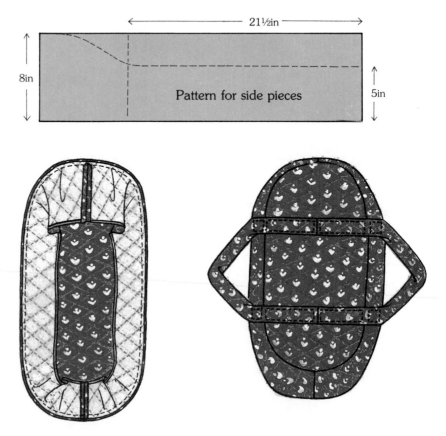

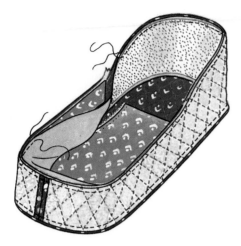

The quilted top cover is sewn to the sides (above), and zippers are put in along both side edges, protected by zipper guards. The sides and top cover are lined and the head section interfaced.

The most suitable fabrics for the carry cot are coordinating fabrics in primary colors or strong pastels (below).

Inserting the zippers

Clip into the seam allowance at each side of top cover where the base of the zippers will be. Pin, baste and stitch top cover to sides around bottom edge from notch to notch, with a ⅝in seam. Pin, baste and stitch one half of each zipper to top cover from notch to top edge. Turn under edges and catch top cover lining down over back of each zipper.

Cut two pieces of contrasting fabric each 19½in by 6¼in for zipper guards. Fold each piece in half lengthwise with right sides together. Pin, baste and stitch shorter edges. Turn right side out. Pin and baste second half of zippers to side pieces. Pin and baste zipper guards over zippers, matching raw edges of guards and side pieces.

Place side lining pieces with right sides together; pin, baste and stitch top and bottom seams, with ⅝in seams. With right sides together and raw edges matching, place side lining over zipper guards. Matching seams at top and bottom, pin and baste in place. Pin, baste and stitch interfacing pieces together at top seam. Place it around head section on the wrong side of the lining, matching top seams.

Pin, baste and stitch all around the top of the side edge, catching in zippers, zipper guards, side lining, interfacing at head section and top cover lining around base edge.

Finishing the lining

With carry cot inside out and raw edges matching, pin, baste and stitch base lining to lower edge of side lining with a ⅝in seam and leaving a 12in opening at the bottom edge. Turn right side out. Turn under opening edges and slip stitch together by hand. Topstitch around head section from top of one zipper to top of second zipper. Place mattress, foam side up, inside carry cot.

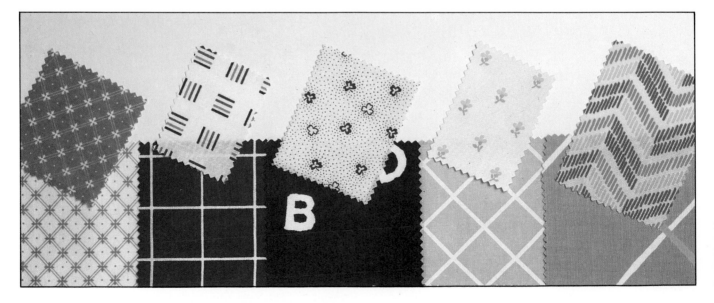

BABY CARRIER

Make a colorful back carrier for a small baby. It leaves the parent's hands free while keeping the baby in close contact.

This practical back carrier, which lets a baby view the world from high up, incorporates a padded headrest and quilted, bound edges to prevent chafing. All seams are stitched twice for extra strength.

A ¼in seam allowance should be added to the headrest, and ⅝in seam allowances to the other pieces.

Cutting out
Cut the pieces to the sizes shown on the cutting layout below, adding on ⅝in seam allowances (except for the headrest, which should have a ¼in seam allowance). Cut a second headrest piece from the quilted fabric. Shape center panels by curving short edges in by ¾in at center.

Making and attaching the straps
Baste center panel pieces together with wrong sides facing.
Mark the center of each long edge on the main straps. Fold under ½in for 10in each side of the center, then fold each strap in half lengthwise with wrong sides together.
Place the straight edges of the center panel between the folded edges of the main straps, baste and zig-zag stitch.

You will need
1yd of 45in-wide cotton canvas or similar strong fabric
½yd of 45in-wide quilted fabric
Thread
2in-wide buckle
Metal eyelets

Cutting layout

20in	20in	4in	
center panel (12in)	center panel	shoulder strap 18in	
main strap (12in)	headrest (8in) (12in)		36in
32in			
main strap (12in)	belt strap (4in)	shoulder strap 18in	
	belt strap (4in)		
fabric 45in wide			

Curve the remaining length at each end of the main straps to reduce them to 2in when folded. Open them out and, with right sides together, stitch the shoulder straps to each end of the top main strap and the belt straps to the ends of the bottom main strap. Refold straps as before.

Binding the edges
Cut bias strips 4½in wide from quilting and bind the curved edges of the center panel up to the seams on the straps. Fold under remaining raw edges of straps for ¼in, enclosing the ends of binding, and machine stitch the folds together.

Finishing the belt straps
Attach a buckle to one belt strap and insert eyelets on the other strap to form a belt. Try on the carrier and fasten the buckle. Bring the shoulder straps over your shoulders and loop around the belt straps. Adjust to allow room for the baby. Turn in the ends and stitch firmly in a rectangle to the wrong side of the shoulder straps.

Making the headrest
Shape the pieces for the headrest by curving in the long edges so bottom edge measures 6in. Round off the top corners. Stitch the two headrest pieces together with right sides together, making ¼in seam and leaving the bottom edge open. Turn right side out, fold under the bottom edges for ⅜in and baste together. Topstitch ⅜in from the edge.
Place the headrest, with quilted side facing up, on the wrong side of the carrier so that the bottom edge is ⅝in below the main strap and the centers are aligned. Zig-zag stitch firmly in position across the bottom.

The baby carrier consists of a double-thickness center panel with main straps attached at the top and bottom. Belt straps are sewn onto the bottom main strap (below left) and shoulder straps to the top main strap. The curved edges are bound, and a quilted headrest is attached just below the top main strap (below right).

You will need

For a sling to fit a baby younger than 3 months

⅞yd of 45in-wide nylon ciré
½yd of 36in-wide terrycloth
½yd of 36in-wide lightweight batting
Two "D" rings or buckles
Three Velcro dots
½yd of ¼in-wide elastic
½yd of 1½in-wide elastic
6¼in by 10in piece of buckram
Thread

Worn in front of the parent and leaving the parent's hands free, a baby sling is the ideal way to carry a young baby.

Most babies like being carried in a baby sling, which is worn in front, where the baby is comforted by the parent's heartbeat. Made from nylon ciré, with terrycloth lining and a lightweight padding, this baby sling has elasticized sides and a stiff headrest, making it suitable even for the newborn.

⅜in seam allowances are included throughout unless otherwise specified.

Cutting out

Enlarge the graph pattern shown on page 84. Cut out these pattern pieces and the straps shown in the measurement diagram below. Cut from main fabric, batting and terrycloth (you will need one each of the straps, from main fabric), marking all dots.

Making and attaching leg straps

With right sides together, fold leg straps in half lengthwise. Stitch down long raw edges. Turn leg straps right side out.

Insert 8in of elastic along the length of straps, and stitch across one end of leg strap to hold elastic in place. Baste a strap each side of terrycloth body between dots.

Making the body

Fold gussets diagonally, wrong sides together. Baste to right side of terrycloth body at corners, matching dots and with raw edges even.

Sandwich terrycloth between batting and main fabric as follows: place the two layers of padding at the bottom, the terrycloth with right side up next, and finally position the outer fabric on top, wrong side up.

Stitch down the long sides of the body and around the leg curves, leaving top and bottom edges open. Trim seams to ¼in and clip leg curves. Turn right side out and press.

Slide a 10in piece of ¼in elastic inside, against the seams of side edges between straps and gussets. Topstitch one end of elastic, then continue topstitching down sides to leg straps. Pull up elastic till gathers measure 4in and pin at open end to hold elastic. Secure by stitching across elastic to edge. Trim off excess elastic and repeat on other side of body.

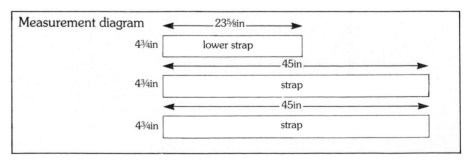

Measurement diagram

4¾in	lower strap	23⅝in
4¾in	strap	45in
4¾in	strap	45in

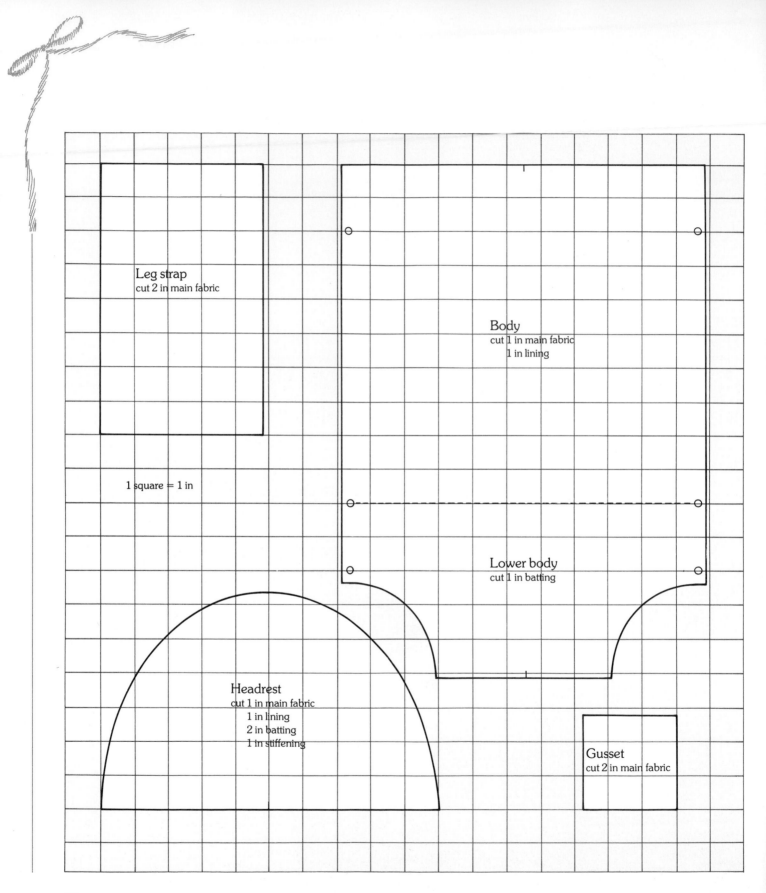

Leg strap
cut 2 in main fabric

Body
cut 1 in main fabric
1 in lining

1 square = 1 in

Lower body
cut 1 in batting

Headrest
cut 1 in main fabric
1 in lining
2 in batting
1 in stiffening

Gusset
cut 2 in main fabric

Making and attaching the top strap and lower strap

Join the two long strips of top strap and press open. On wrong side, center 2in by 16in batting strip across seamline and pin. Baste ends. Fold strap in half lengthwise, right sides together. Leaving 16in open at center, pin, baste and stitch across short ends and down long edges. Trim batting to seamline; turn right side out. Place open edge of top strap on top of body, fabric sides together. Stitch, leaving top edge of strap free. Trim seam then turn under remaining raw edge and topstitch.

Fold lower strap in half lengthwise, right sides together. Baste 2in by 16in piece of batting strip along its length. Stitch across ends and for 6in down one long edge from each end. Trim batting to seamline, then turn strap right side out. Match center of lower strap opening to center of lower body. Pin. Pull up free end of elastic on leg straps until gathers measure 4in. Baste. Stitch leg straps to lower strap, placing inside edge of leg straps 3in from the lower body, along lower strap. Fold under remaining raw edge, then stitch along the lower strap close to edge. Pass strap end through "D" ring; fold back 1¼in. Pin and double stitch ¼in from ends.

Making the headrest

For headrest, sandwich fabrics together as for body. Stitch around curved edge. Trim off ⅜in seam allowance from all around headrest. Trim and clip curve on headrest then turn right side out. Insert stiffener between fabric and batting. Turn under raw edges. Slip stitch. Stitch three Velcro dots to the fabric side of the headrest, one at center and one at each corner, then sew corresponding pieces to center inside of top strap.

After the sling is tied loosely on the parent, the baby should be laid on a bed, with the parent bending over to put it in the sling. When the baby is in place, the straps are tightened as necessary.

OLDER BABY'S SLING

You will need

For a sling to fit a baby age 3 months or older

1⅛yd of 45in-wide or 1⅜yd of 36in-wide corduroy or other fabric

¾yd of 45in-wide contrasting fabric

20in open-ended zipper

Two buckles or "D" rings

Thread

Until a baby starts walking, a baby sling is a useful alternative to a baby carriage or stroller.

This baby sling, made of warm, lined corduroy, is spaciously designed for an infant of three months or older, who does not need as much support as a newborn baby. It is worn with the top straps passing over the parent's shoulders, crossing at the back then passing through the buckles at the side before being firmly tied waist-high at the back.

⅜in seam allowances are included throughout unless otherwise specified.

Cutting out

Enlarge the pattern pieces shown in the graph pattern on pages 88-9. Cut out these pieces along with the straps, lower band and side tabs shown in the measurement diagram below. Cut out from main fabric (allowing for nap if using corduroy) and lining; you will need two tabs, one lower band and one strap in the main fabric. Mark guide lines.

Making the front

With right sides together, stitch lining to front at upper and curved side edge. Trim seam and repeat for other front.

Press ⅜in to wrong side along opening edges of each front and lining, and baste. Turn fronts right side out. Pin basted edges close to zipper teeth on each side of the zipper tape, turning down excess tape on upper edge of zipper and basting carefully. Baste and then stitch fronts and linings to zipper, leaving 2in open below base of zipper.

On upper edges of fronts, match dots to make stitched pleats. Pin, baste and stitch pleats.

Make unstitched pleats on lower edges of fronts by matching small dots to large dots toward side edges. Baste lower-front edge to hold pleats in position.

Making the back

With right sides together, pin, baste and stitch lining to back, leaving lower edge open. Trim seams and clip curves. Turn right side out and press.

Stitch straps together in pairs, leaving 4in open at centers. Trim and turn right side out. Turn under opening edges and slip stitch. Baste straps to back along marked lines. Stitch straps to back by topstitching ⅛in from all edges and along their length. Make tabs for straps. Topstitch edges then slide on buckle, fold in half and, using zipper foot on machine, stitch close to bar.

Turn under ⅜in to wrong side along unnotched edge of lower band, press and baste.

With right sides together, pin, baste and stitch band to lower back edge. Trim seam and press toward band. Fold band in half along its length and stitch ends together. Trim seams then turn right side out. Place basted edge over seam line on front; topstitch, enclosing lower edges.

Measurement diagram

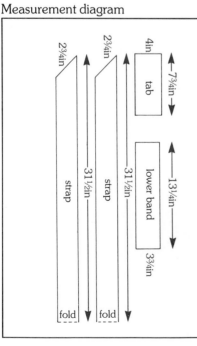

2¾in

2¾in

2¾in

4in

tab

7¾in

31½in

31½in

31½in

strap

strap

lower band

13¼in

3¾in

fold

fold

Finishing the sling
To finish sling, pin upper front corners to back, matching stitching lines.
Stitch triangle. Insert side tabs between back and front at marked points
and stitch in place.

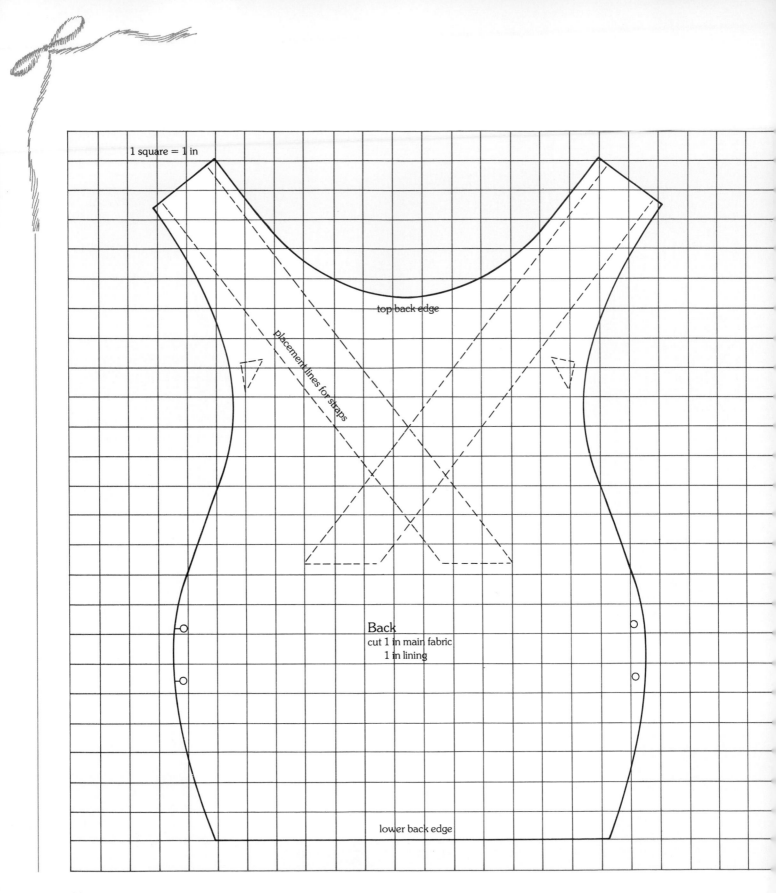

1 square = 1 in

top back edge

placement lines for straps

Back
cut 1 in main fabric
1 in lining

lower back edge

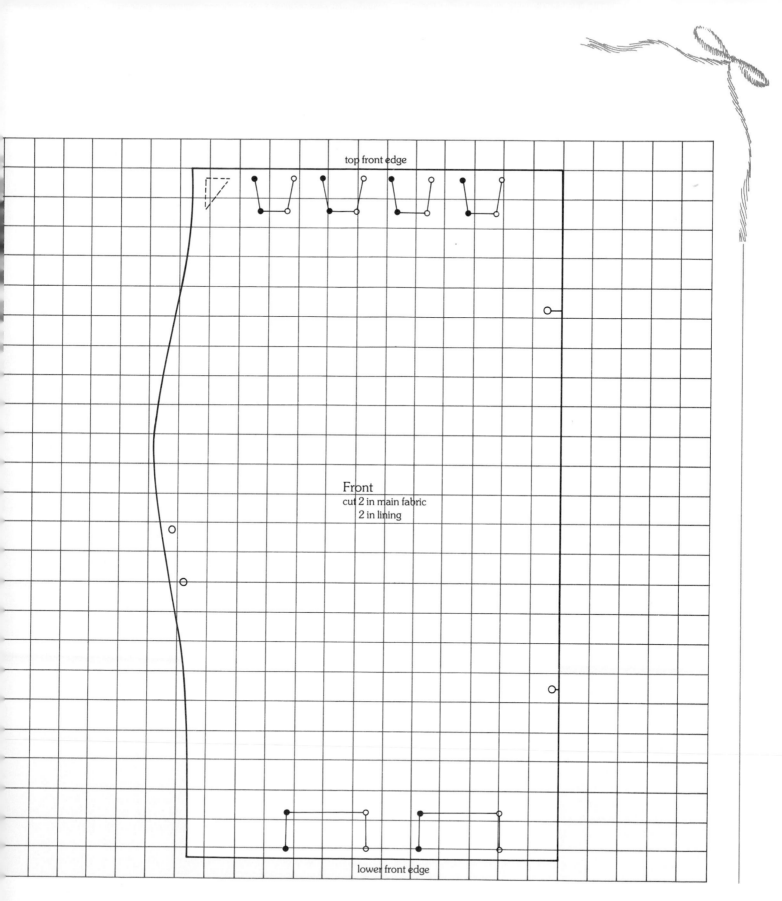

top front edge

Front
cut 2 in main fabric
2 in lining

lower front edge

QUILTED BABY BOUNCER

Give a baby an attractive new bouncing chair by recovering an old one in bright fabric, then add a detachable footwarmer.

Bouncing chairs are wonderful for young babies, providing the support they need and at the same time propping them up so they can view the world. (A bouncing chair should never be placed on a raised surface such as a table, however.) They can be used from the very first weeks until the baby is able to sit up on its own.

Because the covers for bouncing chairs become well worn before the frames, replacing the cover is a worthwhile job that can be done simply and easily. Use the old cover as a pattern and choose a ready-quilted fabric, which will give extra padding to the seat. The finished areas of the bouncing chair are quite small, especially the front strap, so avoid a large print fabric.

The footwarmer is optional but very useful, since small babies can get cold when they lie still. It is neatly secured to the frame with two tape loops at each side which anchor it to the front strap buttons.

⅝in seam allowances are included throughout unless otherwise specified.

Making the pattern and cutting out the cover
Remove the old cover from the frame and undo each part. Cut off all seam allowances, and press each piece flat. These pieces can now be used as a pattern.

Lay pieces on fabric and cut one main piece, one foot piece, one back facing (7in long and with the side shaped following the front cover) and one front strap, adding ⅝in seam allowance all around and 1½in to side edges of main piece. (Be careful to position the pattern so the design runs up the cover and so the design is positioned well on the front parts of the cover.)

Sewing the back facing and main piece of the cover
Finish the bottom straight edge of the back facing by zig-zagging along the edge.

Fold main front piece in half at base, right sides together, to form a dart in base. Pin, baste and stitch dart, graduating the stitching to a point. Finish the raw edges of dart together with zig-zag stitching.

Turn under ⅝in around curved edges on each side of main front piece. Pin, baste and zig-zag stitch turned-under edges down, beginning at straight side edge and ending at base.

Position facing at top edge of main front piece, with right sides together and raw edges even; pin, baste and stitch around curved edge. Trim. Turn facing to wrong side.

Turn side edges under 1½in down both sides of main piece, from just under facing to curved edges. Pin, baste and zig-zag stitch both edges to form casings for frame. Be sure to secure the stitching firmly at the top and bottom so that when the metal frame is slotted in, the stitching will not unravel at all.

You will need
Quilted furnishing cotton
Two ¾in-diameter buttons
⅜in-wide cotton tape
Thread

Sewing the foot piece and front strap of the cover

Zig-zag stitch long sides and back short edge of foot piece. Fold foot piece in half so back edge is 2in from front. Stitch side seams. Zig-zag stitch each side of foot piece, continuing stitching up to raw front edge. Trim off excess fabric. Fold side edges above finished edge to wrong side; stitch.

Turn under all edges of front strap, except base edge; pin, baste and zig-zag stitch. Pin base edges of strap together. Find center of base edges of strap and position in the center over dart on front main piece only. Pin, baste and stitch strap in place.

Place raw front edge of foot piece at base front edge of main piece with right sides together, sandwiching base edges of front strap in between. Stitch together.

Fitting the cover on the frame

Place cover over frame, feeding the main frame down the side casings from under the facing, then pushing in the foot piece and fitting the frame together. Take the strap to the back of the cover and mark positions of the holding buttons and buttonholes. Remove cover; sew on a button at each position. Make a buttonhole in marked positions on the front strap. Make another buttonhole beyond the first one on each side so that the cover can be expanded.

Making the footwarmer

Measure the length of the front from the top of the front strap to the base of the metal frame, adding a good allowance for ease. Double this length, and add 1⅛in for top hems. For the width, measure from side to side, again adding fabric for ease. Cut out one piece to this size.

Fold in half, right sides together, raw edges matching. Pin, baste and stitch from folded base edge to within 10¼in of top.

Zig-zag stitch seam allowance on side edges, continuing stitching up the raw edges on each side. Turn under open edges in line with side seams. Pin, baste and stitch in place.

To form base, fold side seams over center of base, until it measures 5in. Pin, baste and stitch across each side of base. Trim off close to stitching. Zig-zag raw edges.

Cut tape into four 4¾in lengths. Fold each piece in half to form a loop and position at top raw edge, ¾in from sides. Turn over edges; pin, baste and zig-zag stitch.

Slip footwarmer over foot piece and up on either side of the seat. Fix the front loop over the button, then the back loop to hold in place.

APPLIQUÉD BABY BOUNCER

Any baby will love a baby bouncer decorated with bright and cheerful appliqué motifs like these.

This charming baby bouncer will keep a baby safe and happy whether out in the yard or indoors. It consists of a metal frame covered with strong cotton decorated with an appliqué design. The cover – made of two layers of fabric with batting in between – is quilted by hand around the edge of each motif. Choose a small pattern such as a polkadot or a plain fabric for the background, and bright-colored scraps of cotton for the appliqué motifs.

⅝in seam allowances are included throughout unless otherwise specified.

Cutting out the main pieces

If you have the old cover, simply undo it and measure the pieces. If you don't have it, then measure the frame in the following way. Measure from the head to the bottom of the seat section where it joins the footrest, and from side to side at the widest point. Add 1¼in to the length for seam allowances and 6¼in to the width for channels encasing the frame and a dart at the bottom to form the seat. (Allow a bit extra around the head section and sides for ease of working.) Cut out one piece of fabric to this size.

Fold the main piece in half lengthwise with right sides together; pin and baste an 8in-long dart from the fold to the bottom edge 2in away from the fold.

Place the fabric on the frame, right side out, and fold the side edges around the frame up to the point where it starts to curve; pin in place and mark the stitching lines with dressmaker's chalk on both back and front of the fabric. Trim the fabric to size, leaving a ⅝in seam allowance around the top edge and along the bottom, and remove from the frame.

Use this piece to cut out a second fabric piece and one piece of batting. Stitch the dart on all three pieces.

Making the appliqué design

Using dressmaker's graph paper, enlarge the motifs in the graph pattern on page 96 to the right size and cut out the pattern pieces. Cut out appliqué motifs from brightly colored fabrics. Place one main piece on the frame and arrange the appliqué motifs on the fabric to produce a pleasing design; pin in place. Remove the cover from the frame, baste and stitch in a wide, close zig-zag with matching thread.

Stitching the side channels

Place the two main fabric pieces together right sides of the fabric out and with the batting in between. Make sure the darts match exactly. Baste the layers together at 4in intervals and around the edges. Turn ¼in to the wrong side along each edge; pin and baste. Place on frame again to check fit.

Remove and pin, baste and stitch the channels, ending 4in above the

You will need

1¾yd of 48in-wide strong cotton such as canvas, unbleached muslin, furnishing cotton, denim or corduroy.
1yd of 36in-wide lightweight synthetic batting
One 1¼in-wide buckle
Scraps of brightly colored cotton
Tissue paper
Thread

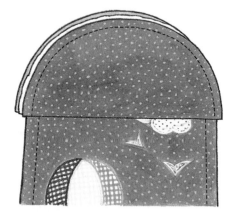

The bouncer is made by first zig-zagging the motifs in position, then sewing the two main fabric pieces together with the batting in between. The pocket is made by stitching the two pocket pieces together, right sides together, with the batting on top (top). This is then stitched around the top edge of the main piece (above).

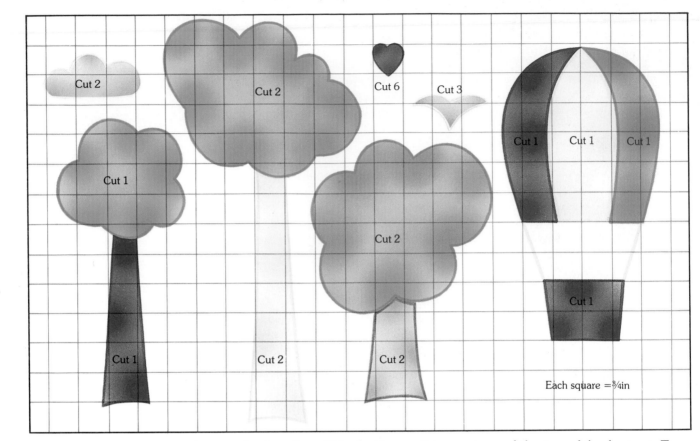

Cut 2

Cut 2

Cut 6

Cut 3

Cut 1

Cut 1   Cut 1   Cut 1

Cut 1

Cut 2

Cut 1

Cut 1

Cut 2   Cut 2

Each square = ¾in

foot section. Trim batting so it tapers toward the top of the footrest. Turn under at raw edges, enclosing the batting, and slip stitch to close.

Preparing the pocket

Using the top end of one main piece as a pattern, cut out two pieces of fabric and one of batting 8in long. Place the two fabric pieces right sides together and put the batting on top; pin and baste along the straight edge. Place a piece of tissue paper on the batting and stitch ⅝in from the straight edge. Trim seam allowances and turn right side out.

Place the pocket piece on the right side of the main piece; pin, baste and stitch around the curved edge ⅝in from the raw edges, tapering toward the side edges where the hood overlaps the side channels. Trim seam allowances and zig-zag the edges together.

Preparing the footrest

Measure the length and width of the footrest section of the frame; double the length and add 1¼in for seam allowances; add 2in to the width for seam allowances. Cut out two pieces of fabric and one of batting.

Place the two fabric pieces with right sides together and the batting on top. Place a piece of tissue paper on the batting and stitch around three edges, leaving one short edge open. Check that the width of the footrest is the same as the bottom of the main section, plus ⅜in at each side. Trim seam allowances and turn right side out.

Sewing the footrest to the main section

Place the foot section on the main section, right sides together and raw edges even. The foot section should extend ⅜in outside each edge of main section. Pin, baste and stitch together ⅝in from the raw edges. Trim the seam allowance of the main section to ¼in, and fold the other one over it to enclose all raw edges. Pin, baste and stitch again.
Fold the footrest to the right side until it meets the seam. Pin, baste and stitch the sides together, with a ⅜in seam. Turn right side out.

Quilting

Using thread that matches the background fabric, sew a line of running stitch all around each appliqué motif, just outside the edge, sewing through all layers.

Making the straps

From the remaining fabric cut three 2¾in wide strips, 4¾in, 10½in and 20in long. Fold each strip in half lengthwise, right sides together. Pin, baste and stitch ⅜in from the long edge. Turn right side out. Turn under ¼in at each raw end and slip stitch to close.
Turn under ⅜in at one end of the longest strap and position it at the back of the main piece, on the seamline, 8in up from the footrest. Pin, baste and stitch in place. Fold the shortest strap in half around the buckle and attach to the opposite side in the same way.
Turn under ⅜in at one end of the third strap, then turn under 1½in, and stitch close to the edge to form a loop. Attach other end as before to center of bottom edge. Thread long strap through loop.

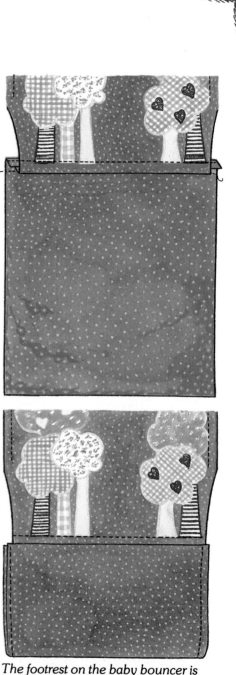

The footrest on the baby bouncer is prepared like the pocket but with three sides stitched. It is stitched to the main piece along the lower edge of the main piece (top). It is then folded to the right side and the side seams are stitched before it is turned right side out (above).

97

BOUNCING SWING

Give a baby's bouncing swing a new seat in a tough cotton fabric. It will keep a baby happy while providing good exercise.

98

A bouncing swing helps a baby to develop leg muscles as he or she bounces up and down. It can be used as soon as the baby can support his/her head. The swing should be suspended in a doorway so that the clamp fixes to each side of the door frame and is held in place by the surrounding wood trim. A baby should never be left unsupervised in a bouncing swing.

Use the strings and clips from the old swing to thread through the new seat, and either use the original beads or buy new.

⅝in seam allowances are included throughout unless otherwise specified.

You will need
¾yd of 36in-wide heavy cotton fabric
Small piece of medium-weight batting
7in of 2in-wide elastic
Jumbo snap kit
Large eyelets and eyelet tool
Four 1in-diameter beads
Thread

Preparing the fabric

Enlarge the graph pattern shown on page 100 and transfer to the fabric.

For the batting, measure between the dashed lines on the pattern and the fold line, and double the measurement. For the straps you will need two pieces of fabric each 6in by 7¾in. The elastic fits between the two strap pieces. The snaps connect the straps to the seat and the eyelets hold the hanging strips.

Making the seat

From fabric cut two seat pieces. From batting cut one piece and place on wrong side of one fabric piece. Stitch seat pieces together at side edges, catching in batting. Trim down the batting on both side edges against the stitching line. Snip into the curved edges of the seam allowance. Turn the seat right side out.

Press the side seams to the edge. Pin, baste and topstitch down the side edges, stitching ⅜in from the outer edge. Repeat to topstitch opposite side edge.

Fold ⅝in on one short edge to wrong side at top leg shaping. Edge stitch in place, then topstitch ¼in from edge stitching. Repeat at opposite edge.

Making the straps

From fabric cut out two straps. Fold one strap in half lengthwise right sides together. Taking ⅝in seam, stitch one short and long edge, leaving remaining edge open. Trim, and turn strap right side out. Turn the raw edges in ⅝in on the remaining short side and pin separately to hold. Repeat to make up second strap.

Take elastic and insert ⅝in of one end of the elastic into open end of one strap piece. To hold elastic in place, stitch across strap close to edge. Repeat to edge stitch second strap to opposite end of elastic. Stitch all around both straps close to outer edge. Stitch across elasticized end, ¼in from previous row.

Assembling the seat

Thread elasticized strap through back section of seat 1½in down from folded edge and pin in the center to hold. Stitch elastic in place down the center. Begin and end the stitching with a few backstitches to hold the strap firmly in place.

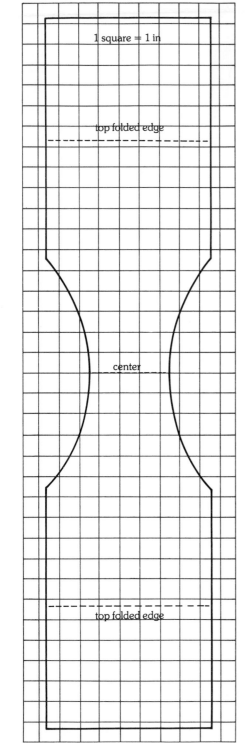

1 square = 1 in

top folded edge

center

top folded edge

Or, instead, sew two rows of stitching close together in a continuous length, overlapping the ends.

Topstitch around seat again, ⅜in from the previous topstitching, then sew another line of stitching straight down the center part of the seat.

Mark positions of the jumbo snaps on front of seat and on each strap. Following pattern, position four top halves on each strap. (The first two should be ⅜in from the front edge and the second two a further 1in away. All four should be ⅜in from the sides of the strap.) Position two base halves on each side of seat.

Mark and fix an eyelet into the top corners of seat pieces, following pattern for positions. Thread with cord and beads.

ZIP-UP CHANGING BAG

Make an attractive baby changing bag that unzips to form a soft, hygienic surface for changing a baby's diapers.

This changing mat has an easy-to-clean top and incorporates a layer of soft foam, with a raised foam ridge all around the edges to help prevent a baby from rolling off. It folds in half in the middle and zips up at the sides to form a roomy bag, with handles for hanging over the shoulder or on a stroller.

⅝in seam allowances are included throughout unless otherwise specified.

You will need
Fabric
Vinyl-coated cotton fabric in matching print
1in-thick foam
Latex glue for foam
Two open-ended zippers
Thread
Paperclips
Clothespins

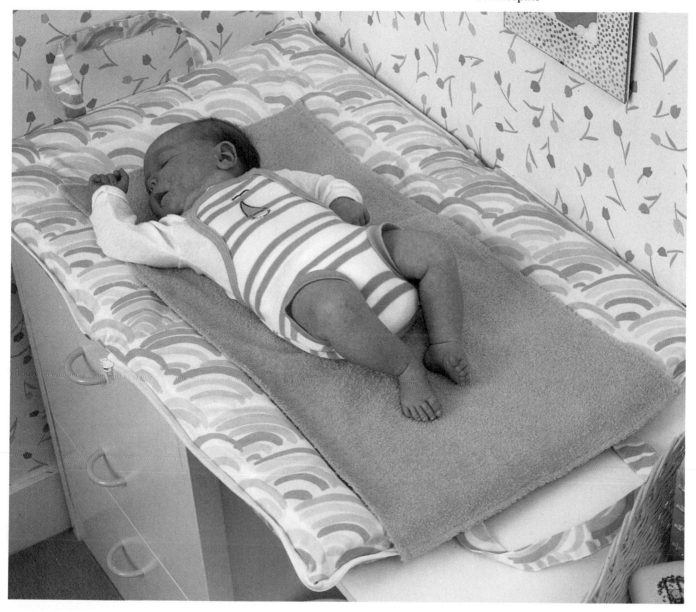

Preparing the foam and fabric

Decide on the size of mat you need, bearing in mind the best size for carrying – it will be folded in half. This will be the size of the foam base. For the raised edges, measure length and width and allow for two side pieces and one end piece, both 3in wide.

For the fabric, measure the length and width of the foam base and add 1¼in seam allowance to both measurements. For handles, allow for sufficient length so the mat can hang either from the shoulder or over the handles of a stroller. For vinyl-coated cotton, measure as above, omitting handles. For length of zippers, measure half the foam length minus 1in.

Before cutting out, iron your fabric on the wrong side with a cool iron to eliminate wrinkles. If you need to iron vinyl-coated cotton on the right side at any time, cover the plastic surface with brown paper first. Always test the heat setting on the iron on a scrap of fabric.

It is not necessary to cut the vinyl-coated cotton according to the direction of the grain, only according to design. Use double-sided tape, not pins, to hold pattern pieces to fabric before cutting out.

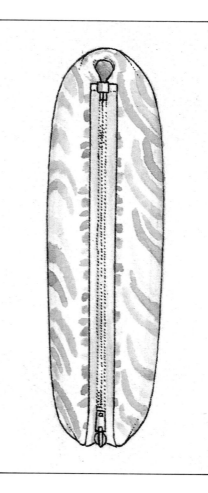

Making the foam base

For base, from foam cut one piece to size. Cut out raised side pieces. Mark V-shape with a 2¼in base in the center on long raised pieces. Cut along marked lines, removing the V-shaped pieces of foam. Position raised sides on top of foam base, matching side edges. Trim end piece to fit between long sides. Stick in place with V-shaped gaps pointing outward.

Making the handles

For handles, from fabric cut two pieces to desired size. On each handle piece, fold in ⅝in seam allowance along each long edge and press in position. Fold handle in half lengthwise, matching folded edges. Topstitch folded edges together. Stitch down other fold to match. Repeat for the second handle.

Assembling the bag

Cut one mat piece from vinyl-coated cotton and one from fabric. Position handle on short edge of fabric mat, with each end 1in in from sides. Stitch. Repeat with second handle at opposite end.

Separate zipper. Stitch half of zipper to one long side of fabric mat. Stitch opposite half to the other end of same side, leaving a gap of 2in between ends. Repeat on opposite side.

Place fabric and vinyl-coated cotton mats with right sides together. Stitch with a ⅝in seam, leaving an opening between handles on one short side. Trim and turn.

Insert foam into bag with raised edges against the vinyl-coated cotton side of the bag. Turn in opening edges and slip stitch together to close. Fit zippers together and close.

FOLD-UP CHANGING BAG

The beauty of this changing bag is that the pockets keep a baby's needs at hand when it is used as a changing mat.

This practical changing mat has a padded center changing area with surrounding panels to help prevent an active baby from rolling off. Each side panel has one deep pocket for diapers and two smaller pockets for other items. The pockets are placed so that they will be right side up when the mat is carried. For carrying, the side panels fold in and tie together at top and bottom corners to support the pockets. Then the top and bottom panels fold in, and the center panel folds in half to form a neat bag complete with handles.

Instead of vinyl-coated cotton inside and out, you could use it just on the inside, then use a sturdy coordinating or contrasting cotton fabric outside. In that case, the outer side and handles will take 1¼yd of 48in-wide fabric; and the inner side and pockets will take 1⅜yd of 48in-wide fabric. The cutting layout on page 106 can be simply divided in two by moving the small pockets down to the cut-out corners of the inner mat.

⅝in seam allowances are included throughout unless otherwise specified.

Cutting out
Following measurement diagram on this page, make a paper pattern for main piece. Following cutting layout on page 106, draw around pattern on wrong side of fabric using dressmaker's chalk to mark out two main pieces, two small pockets 8⅝in-wide by 6in deep, two long pockets 8⅝in-wide by 20in deep, and four handles 21in by 1¼in. Cut out pieces and lightly mark mat stitching line, indicated by dashed line on pattern, onto the right side of main pieces.

Making and attaching the handles
Place two handle pieces together with wrong sides together. Press bias binding in half with upper folded half of binding slightly narrower than under half. Insert each long edge of handle into binding with narrower half of binding up. Stitch in place.

With right sides together, place one handle at each end of outer mat piece, with handle facing toward center of mat and ends even with mat stitching line (in other words, 8in from top/bottom outer edge). Each handle should be centered on the stitching line, with 6¼in between the inner edges of the ends. Stitch across the ends of the handles 1¼in from the raw edge. Trim off ¼in from the ends. Fold each handle over toward the edge of the mat, and stitch to the mat along the mat stitching line, enclosing the raw ends.

Making the pockets
Bind upper long edges of each small pocket, and both short edges of each long pocket by sewing on binding in the same way as straps.

With right sides together, position long pockets on inner mat piece with bottom edges 4in up from mat stitching line. Outer side edge of pockets

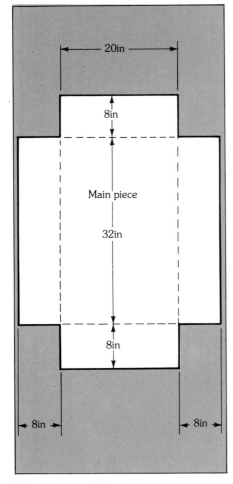

20in

8in

Main piece

32in

8in

8in   8in

Measurement diagram

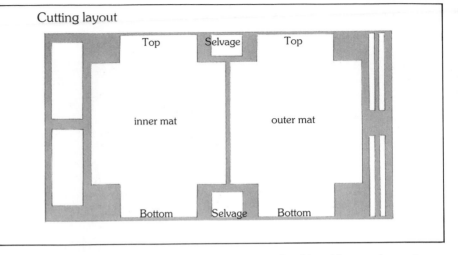

Cutting layout

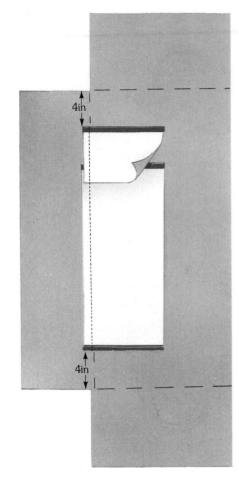

The changing mat pockets are formed by positioning a long pocket and a short pocket together as shown in the top illustration and stitching down one side. The pockets are then folded over and stitched again, at right angles to the previous stitching line.

should extend over the side mat stitching line by ⅝in. Pin in place along mat stitching line.

In the same way pin small pockets with bound edge 4in below top mat stitching line, so lower edge overlaps long pocket by 2in. Stitch the side edges of the pockets to mat along side mat stitching line.

Fold small pockets over toward side edges to cover seam allowances. With outer side edges of pockets and mat level, stitch pocket to mat across lower edge of pocket ⅝in up from raw edge.

In the same way fold long pocket over so outer side edges are even and stitch long pocket to mat across center of side panel, forming a second smaller pocket beneath the first and a large deeper pocket facing in the opposite direction. Stitch the pockets to mat along the outer side edges.

Padding the mat
With the right sides on the outside, sandwich batting in the middle between outer and inner mat. Pin together through all layers at intervals along mat stitching line. Stitch around mat stitching line. Open out panels to trim batting just outside the stitching. Stitch outer edges together near to edge and trim edges even if necessary.

Making the ties and binding the edge
Cut four 14in-long pieces of binding. Press one raw end of each piece to wrong side. With wrong sides together, press bindings in half lengthwise and stitch along both edges. With raw edges even, sew one tie to corner of outer mat at side edge of each side panel with small stitches.

Press remaining binding in same way as with the handles. Insert outer edge of mat into binding, pinning at intervals. Miter binding at outer corners and stretch around inner corners in a curve. Sew ends of binding together to fit. Stitch binding in place, enclosing ends of ties in the stitching. Fold side panels of mat in and fasten ties together at top and bottom before folding the mat, which is now ready for carrying.

TEDDYBEAR BATH SET

These tiny teddies make ideal traveling companions, as well as staying happily at home to delight the family at bathtime.

The baby's bath set consists of a pink towel, a pink washcloth and a blue spongebag (made from two blue washcloths). Each is appliquéd with teddybears cut from a blue towel and pink washcloth. Bows are attached with satin stitch, and the bears' claws and features are embroidered in straight stitch.

3⁄8in seam allowances are included on the sponge bag.

Preparation and cutting out

Trace the teddy outline shown opposite (for washcloth and sponge bag) and enlarge the pattern (for towel). Make an extra copy of the teddy shapes for reference.

Fuse transfer fusing web to the backs of the blue towel and the pink washcloth, avoiding the woven edges of the towel and washcloth. Use carbon paper to transfer two large teddies, one in reverse, and one small teddy onto the backing paper on the blue towel. Transfer two small teddies, one in reverse, onto the pink washcloth. Carefully cut out.

Applying the teddies

Position the two large teddies on the pink towel, setting them level above the towel's woven border. Fuse together. Fuse the small blue teddy to the center of the pink washcloth, and the two pink teddies, one in reverse, on a blue wash cloth, keeping the woven edges at the top and bottom. Draw in the arms, legs and features with marking pen.

To stitch the teddies, use blue thread for the pink teddies, and vice versa. Experiment on a spare piece of towel for the best zig-zag stitch size. Zig-zag around the outlines until the stitches cover the appliqué shapes smoothly and evenly.

Adding the details

Cut the ribbon into 10in lengths and tie these into bows. Attach each bow to the shoulder of a teddy by embroidering satin stitch across the knot. Embroider the facial features and claws in simple straight stitch, and make the mouth line of each bear into a smile.

Making the sponge bag

Make the loops for the cord by cutting four strips, 4in by 2in, from the remains of the blue towel. Fold in half lengthwise and sew down the center with zig-zag stitch. Position two loops 4¾in apart on each blue washcloth, just below the top woven edge. Fold the ends in and sew.

Sew the washcloths together, right sides together, starting and finishing the stitching below the top woven edge, making a 3⁄8in seam. To make a flat base for the bag, pinch across from one side of the lower woven edge to the other at each corner of the bag and stitch. Turn right side out. Cut the cording in half; thread both pieces through loops. Knot ends.

You will need

1 pink guest towel
1 blue guest towel
1 pink washcloth
2 blue washcloths
60in pink cording
30in narrow pink ribbon
20in narrow blue ribbon
Transfer fusing web
Thread
Brown embroidery floss
Fabric marking pen

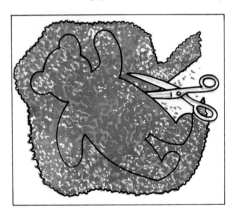

It is important to check the edge of the terrycloth motif for loose fiber after cutting out. Trim away all loose and broken loops before sewing (top). The piece of towel used for the appliqué is first fused to transfer fusing web (above). This makes cutting out easier, and reduces the problem of frayed edges. The towel is easier to handle as well when sewing.

Trace for washcloth
and sponge bag

Enlarge teddy shape
for towel

Each square = ½in

FIRST CLOTHES

Baby clothes are always a popular and welcome gift, and there's a great selection to choose from in this chapter.

The knitting patterns feature a wide variety of garments, both traditional and modern. On page 130 the lacy collection consists of a dress, a matinee jacket and an angel top, together with a luxurious shawl to wrap the baby in, all knitted in a pretty lacy stitch. There are cute leggings with a knitted-in swan motif (page 134), and dainty striped leggings with a very stylish coordinating cardigan (page 140). The ribbed pants and cable top (page 137) would make a fine gift for any baby boy.

For those who crochet, there is a beautiful shawl that is worked in hairpin crochet (page 144). This would be very useful for wrapping around a young baby and would also be perfect for a christening.

Things to sew include little embroidered baby shoes (page 112) which would make a delightful keepsake. On page 114 there is a two-piece outfit, which could be adapted in a number of ways. There's a pair of traditional rompers (page 122) to make up in two coordinating fabrics, and a pretty eyelet sundress (page 119) that could also be made up as a jumper in a different fabric. The sun bonnet on page 117 would look nice with either the rompers or the sundress. Finally, the warm and comfortable sleep suit (page 126) is just right for snuggly bedtime wear.

BABY SHOES

These embroidered shoes are darling on a little baby and make a very special keepsake.

Embroider these pretty fabric shoes for a three month old baby. Use a satin stitch motif and finish with toning binding.
¼in seam allowances are included throughout unless otherwise specified.

Transferring the pattern
Enlarge the graph pattern shown below, and transfer pattern for two shoe tops to denim, using dressmaker's carbon paper. Mark the outline, center line and curved lines at center of top of shoes.

Embroidering and sewing the shoe tops
Trace the embroidery design shown below and center at toes, reversing the motif on second shoe. Transfer using dressmaker's carbon paper and embroider in satin stitch (see page 51). Cut out shoe tops, then cut along center and curved lines to make straps. Hand sew or machine stitch center back with a ¼in seam. Trim one seam allowance to half width, fold the other over it and slip stitch to shoe to make a self-bound seam.

Completing the shoes
Cut out four sole pieces, reversing the pattern for two of them. Match shapes, wrong sides together, and quilt together by hand or machine.
Run a gathering thread between A and B on shoe tops, ¼in from edge. With center backs matching, pin edge of shoe top over edge of sole so top overlaps by ¼in. Hand sew together. Starting at center back, pin bias binding over seam so lower edge just covers edge of shoe top. Hemstitch top edge to shoe, then ease bottom edge so it lies flat.
Clip an opening on right strap of left shoe and left strap of right shoe big enough to take button or bead. Starting at back, fold binding over raw edges of straps and front of shoe, easing around corners. Work buttonhole stitch around openings on straps, stitching through binding, which should enclose raw edges. Sew buttons or beads to the remaining straps.

You will need
For shoes to fit a baby age 3 months
8in by 24in piece of heavyweight brushed denim in beige
1 skein each of Bates Anchor brand stranded cotton embroidery floss shade 0281 (green), 060, 062 and 063 (pink)
1 package pink bias binding
Thread
Two wooden buttons or beads

Key

=0281	=062
=060	=063

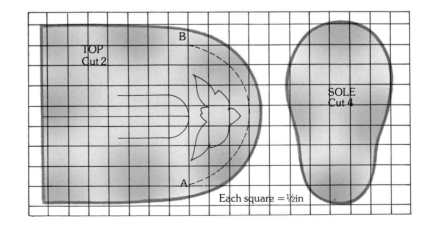

TOP
Cut 2

B

A

SOLE
Cut 4

Each square = ½in

TWO-PIECE OUTFIT

This simple outfit can be made to fit any baby and provides tremendous scope for adaptation.

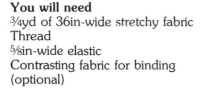

You will need
¾yd of 36in-wide stretchy fabric
Thread
⅝in-wide elastic
Contrasting fabric for binding
(optional)

The pattern pieces for this simple baby outfit are based on rectangles; to add the shaping you just need a ruler and flexible curve. You can make the outfit fit the baby by adjusting the measurements as required. As well as simple adaptations to the pattern pieces such as shortening sleeves and altering the neckline, you can make the top with the opening at the front so that it becomes a coat; substitute loops for the ties and add buttons for a more substantial fastening. Vary the pants by adding a bib with shoulder straps or by shortening the legs to make knickers. ⅝in seam allowances should be added to the measurement diagram.

Cutting out
Draw the pattern as shown in the measurement diagram opposite, adding ⅝in seam allowances all around. Cut out on double fabric, placing shoulder lines on fold and following the cutting layout. From spare or contrasting fabric cut bias strips 2in wide for binding plus a patch pocket 4in by 3in (optional).

Making the top
With right sides together, join the front to the back at the underarms and sides. Press.
Bind the hem and center back edges with a long continuous strip. Bind the ends of the sleeves.
Cut binding to fit neck plus 20in. Fold binding in half lengthwise, right sides together; stitch across short ends and, from both ends, for 10in toward center making ¼in seams. Fit neck edge into remaining part of binding, turn ties right side out and finish neck.
Cut two more 10in pieces of binding and fold in half lengthwise with right sides together. Stitch across one end and down length along foldline on bought bias binding or making ¼in seams on cut bias. Turn right side out. Sew on ties halfway down center back.
Bind the edges of the pocket and stitch it in position on the front of the top.

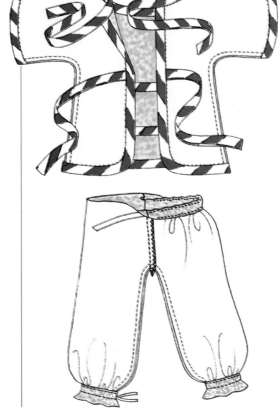

Making the pants
With right sides together, stitch the inner leg seams of each pants leg. Turn one leg right side out and slip it inside the other leg with right sides together. Stitch the seam from center front waist to center back waist and press.
Turn up ¼in and a 1½in hem at the bottom of each leg and stitch, leaving ⅝in open to insert elastic. Work a second row of stitching below the first.
At the waist turn under ¼in and then ⅞in hem and stitch, leaving ⅝in open. Make a second row of stitching along the top fold.
Insert elastic into each casing, draw up to fit, stitch the ends together and stitch the opening closed.

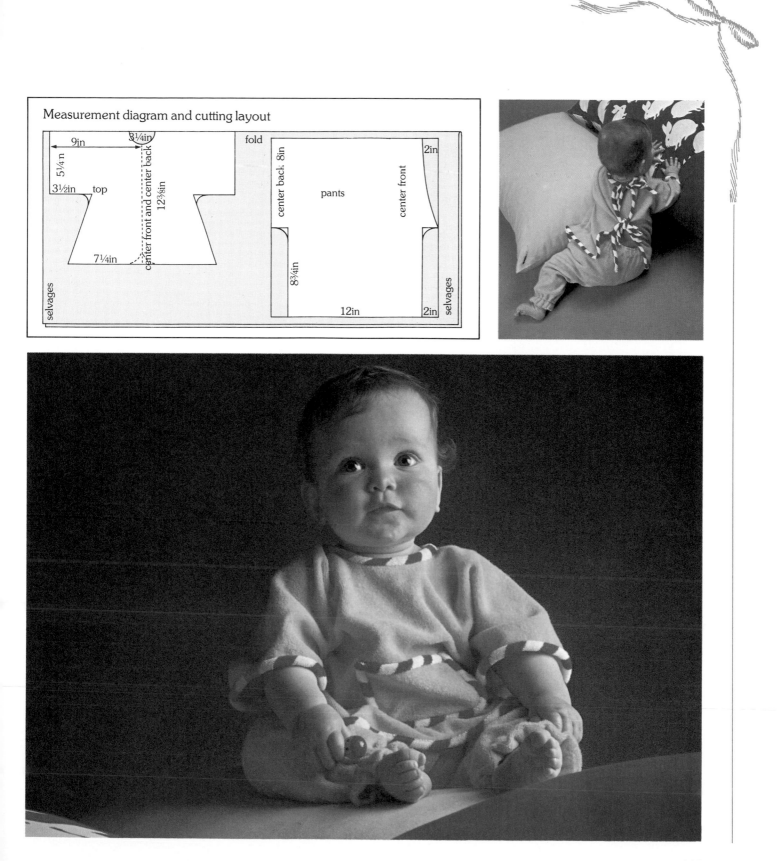

Measurement diagram and cutting layout

SUN BONNET

This little eyelet sun bonnet not only looks cute, it also provides some protection on sunny days.

Quick and easy to make, the bonnet consists of three main pieces gathered onto a band that ties under the chin. It is trimmed with lace or a fabric ruffle and lined with the same fabric. (The dress pattern and directions appear on pages 119-21.)
⅜in seam allowances are included throughout unless otherwise specified.

Cutting out
Enlarge the graph pattern on page 118 and cut out the pieces as shown in the cutting layout on this page. If using lace trim, omit the ruffle pattern piece. Transfer the pattern markings to the fabric.

Sewing together the main bonnet pieces
Matching snips, stitch two side pieces to bonnet center. Press seams toward center. Topstitch ¼in from seams. Stitch other two side pieces and center piece together in same way, omitting topstitching, to form lining.

Making a fabric ruffle (optional)
To make a gathered ruffle from fabric, fold the ruffle piece in half lengthwise with wrong sides together, and press. With raw edges even, stitch two rows of gathering stitches along the raw edges within the seam allowance. Pull up the gathers evenly.

Attaching the ruffle or lace trim
If using flat lace, first gather the edge and pull up to measure 20in. With raw edges even, baste the fabric ruffle or gathered lace to right side of bonnet front (the edge without snips).

Lining the bonnet
With right sides together, stitch lining to bonnet at front edge, sandwiching the ruffle in the seam.
Press lining to inside.
Topstitch ¼in in from front edge.
Baste lower edges together; gather between snips.

Adding the band
Matching snips, pin band to lower edge. Pull up gathers to fit, arrange evenly and stitch.
Fold ends of band in half lengthwise with right sides together. Stitch across ends and along long edges to meet ends of previous stitching. Trim corners.
Turn band ends right side out and press. Turn under free edge along center part of band and slip stitch into back of previous stitching on inside of bonnet. Topstitch ¼in in around band.

You will need
For a baby age 3 to 6 months
Bonnet with lace trim
½yd of 36in-wide eyelet or cotton, or ⅜yd of 45in-wide eyelet or cotton
Thread
⅝yd of 2in-wide gathered lace or 1⅛yd of flat lace
Bonnet with fabric ruffle
⅝yd of 36in-wide eyelet or cotton, or ½yd of 45in-wide eyelet or cotton
Thread

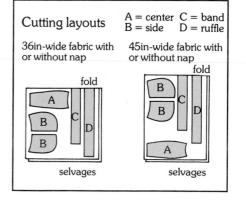

Cutting layouts   A = center   C = band
                     B = side   D = ruffle

36in-wide fabric with or without nap   45in-wide fabric with or without nap

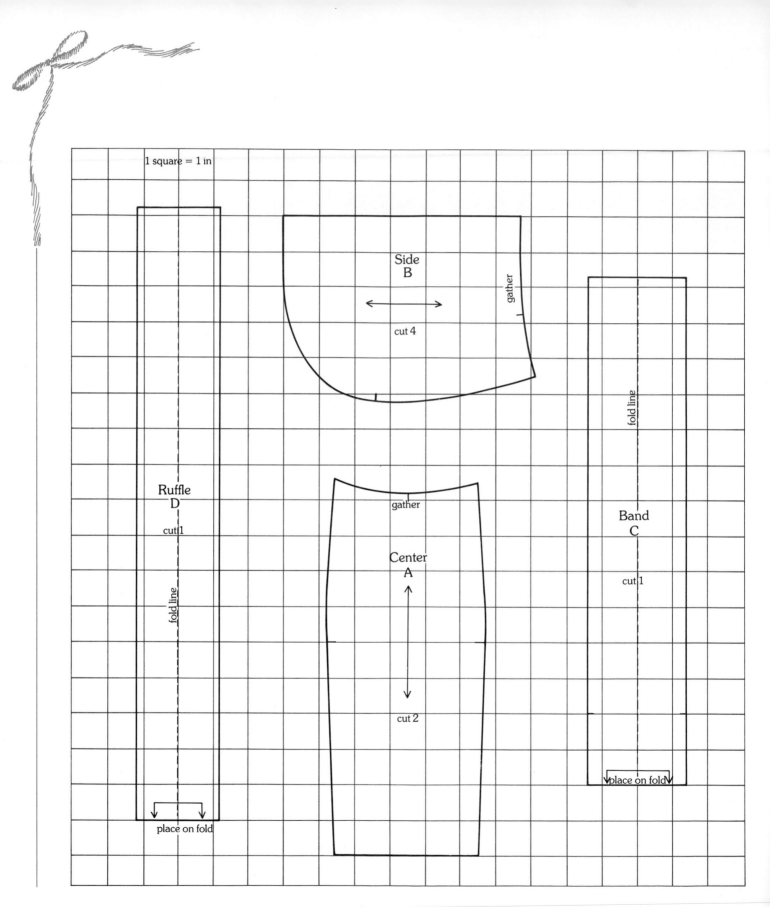

1 square = 1 in

Side
B

gather

cut 4

Ruffle
D

cut 1

fold line

place on fold

Center
A

gather

cut 2

Band
C

fold line

cut 1

place on fold

SUNDRESS

Here's a perfect dress for summer days. Made in a lightweight cotton such as eyelet, it is cool and easy-fitting.

Decorated with tucks and lace trim, this comfortable sundress has a bound neckline and armholes. It buttons at the shoulders and is easy to slip on and off.

⅜in seam allowances are included throughout unless otherwise specified.

Cutting out
Enlarge the graph pattern on page 121 and cut out the pieces as shown in the cutting layout on this page. (Cut the front wider than the pattern then recut accurately after stitching pin tucks.) Cut 1in-wide bias strips as indicated to make a total length of 44in. Transfer the pattern markings to the fabric.

Making the tucks
Mark center tuck line by folding front piece in half and pressing. Unfold and stitch along crease line, using a twin needle; stitch four more tucks on either side, with each tuck the presser foot's width away from the previous tuck.

If you don't have a twin-needle machine, straight stitch tucks by folding front in half with wrong sides together, pressing and then stitching near the fold; press and stitch four more tucks on either side of the first tuck, about ⅜in apart.

Making the straps
Finish the straight shoulder edges of front straps and press onto wrong side along the foldline.

To reinforce end of straps, from leftover fabric cut two pieces to the shape of the ends of the back straps with the fabric selvage placed along dashed line on pattern.

Baste to wrong side of straps.

Stitching side seams and binding edges
Matching snips, stitch front to back at side seams. Finish edges together and press to one side.

Finishing at top of front straps, stitch bias strip around neck and armhole edges, making a ¼in seam.

Fold edge of strip over to wrong side. Tuck under raw edge and ends and slip stitch into back of machine stitching.

Finishing the sundress
Make buttonholes at positions marked on back straps. Sew buttons to front straps to correspond.

Stitch lace around lower edge with right sides together, and raw edges even. Finish the edges together and press upward. Topstitch close to the seam to keep the trim down.

You will need
For a dress measuring approximately 12½in from shoulder, to fit a baby age 3 to 6 months
1yd of 36in-wide or ¾yd of 45in-wide lightweight cotton
Two ⅜in-diameter buttons
1⅛yd of narrow gathered lace
Thread

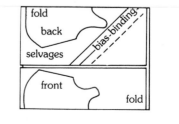

Cutting layout

36/45in-wide fabric with or without nap

fold
back
selvages
bias binding

front
fold

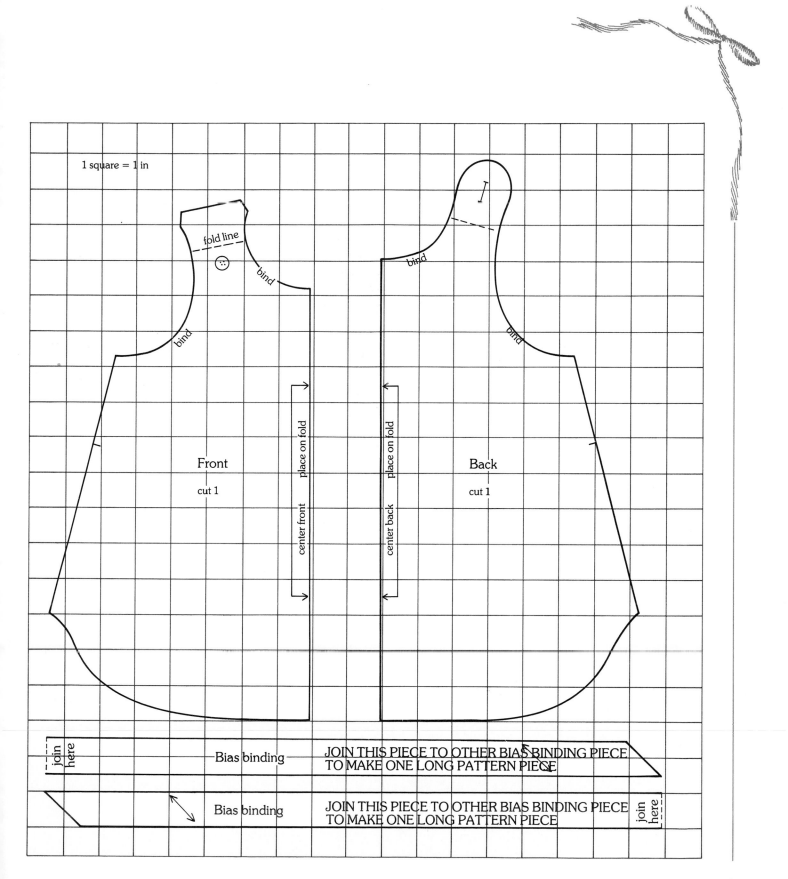

1 square = 1 in

fold line

bind

bind

Front

cut 1

place on fold

center front

bind

bind

Back

cut 1

place on fold

center back

join here

Bias binding

JOIN THIS PIECE TO OTHER BIAS BINDING PIECE
TO MAKE ONE LONG PATTERN PIECE

Bias binding

JOIN THIS PIECE TO OTHER BIAS BINDING PIECE
TO MAKE ONE LONG PATTERN PIECE

join here

Rompers

Perfect for playtime, these rompers allow plenty of freedom of movement for even the most active baby.

These traditional rompers with elasticized legs have bound edges around the top. The shoulder straps have button fastenings, and the front is decorated with a pocket edged in matching binding. The bodice and pants can be made in the same or coordinating fabric.
³⁄₈in seam allowances are included throughout unless otherwise specified.

You will need
For rompers measuring approximately 14in in length, to fit a baby age 3 to six months
¾yd of 36in-wide or 45in-wide poplin, piqué, chambray, soft denim, polyester satin or other light- to medium-weight fabric, for pants
⅝yd of 36in-wide or 45in-wide fabric as above, for bodice
⅓yd of 36in-wide or 45in-wide fabric for binding
1⅛yd of narrow elastic
Two ³⁄₈in-diameter buttons
Thread
Motif (optional)

Cutting out
Enlarge the graph pattern on pages 124-5 and cut out the pieces as shown in the cutting layout on this page. Transfer the pattern markings to the fabric. Cut 1in-wide bias strips as indicated and sew together to make a total length of 63in.

Making the bodice
Easing binding around curves, stitch bias strip around top and side edges of pocket, making a ¼in seam. Fold edge of strip over to wrong side. Tuck under raw edge and ends and slip stitch into back of machine stitching.
Baste pocket to right side of one bodice front. Stitch sides just inside binding and at stitching lines.
With right sides together and raw edges even, stitch one back bodice to the front bodice at side seams. Stitch other bodice pieces in same way to form bodice lining.
Baste the two together around outer edges. Bind neck and armhole edge of bodice as with the pocket.

Making the pants
With right sides together and raw edges even, stitch the two pants pieces together at center front and center back seams. Zig-zag the edges together and press to one side.
With right sides together and matching center seams, stitch crotch seam in same way.

Finishing the rompers
Stitch two rows of gathering threads within the seam allowance of upper edge of pants. Draw up gathers to fit lower edge of bodice. Matching centers and dots on pants to bodice side seams, stitch pants to bodice. Zig-zag edges together and press the seam allowance up.
Turn under ¼in and then ⅝in around legs. Stitch close to the turned-under edge to form casings for the elastic, leaving a gap in the stitching on each leg to thread the elastic. Insert the elastic and adjust to fit. Overlap elastic ends and sew securely. Stitch along gaps in stitching.
Make buttonholes at positions marked on back bodice straps. Sew on buttons to correspond on front bodice straps. Hand sew motif to center of pocket if desired.

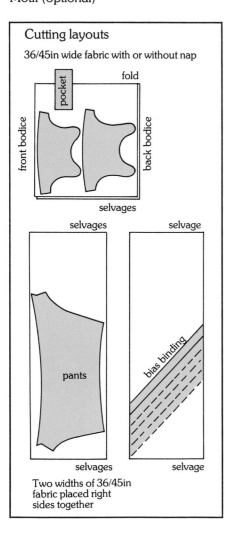

Cutting layouts

36/45in wide fabric with or without nap

fold

pocket

front bodice

back bodice

selvages

selvages · selvage

pants

bias binding

selvages · selvage

Two widths of 36/45in fabric placed right sides together

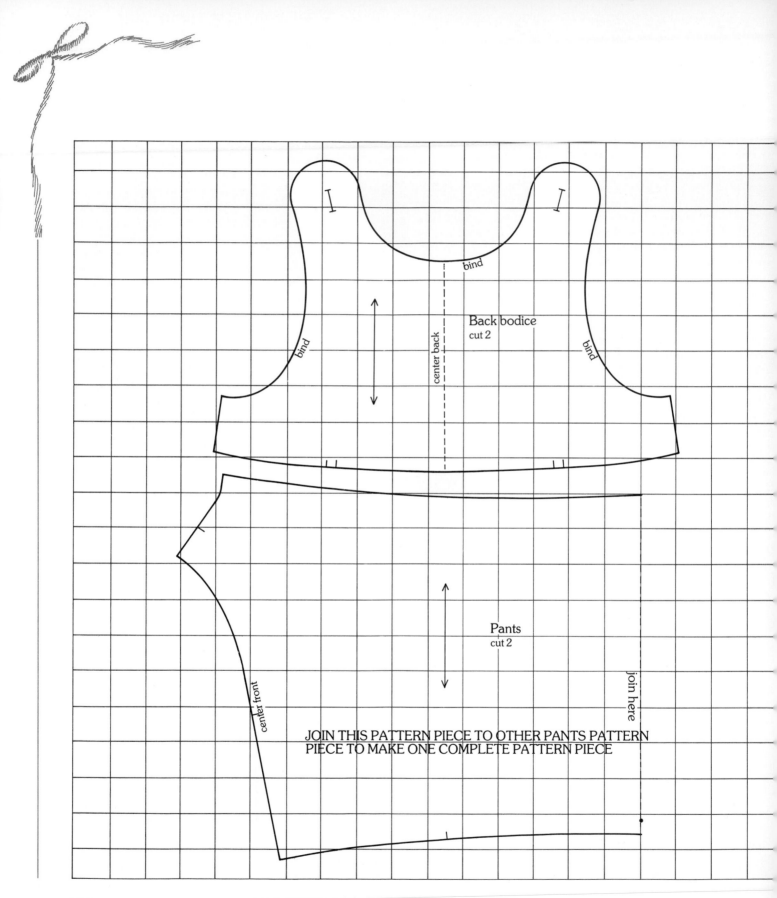

Back bodice
cut 2

bind

bind

bind

center back

Pants
cut 2

center front

join here

JOIN THIS PATTERN PIECE TO OTHER PANTS PATTERN
PIECE TO MAKE ONE COMPLETE PATTERN PIECE

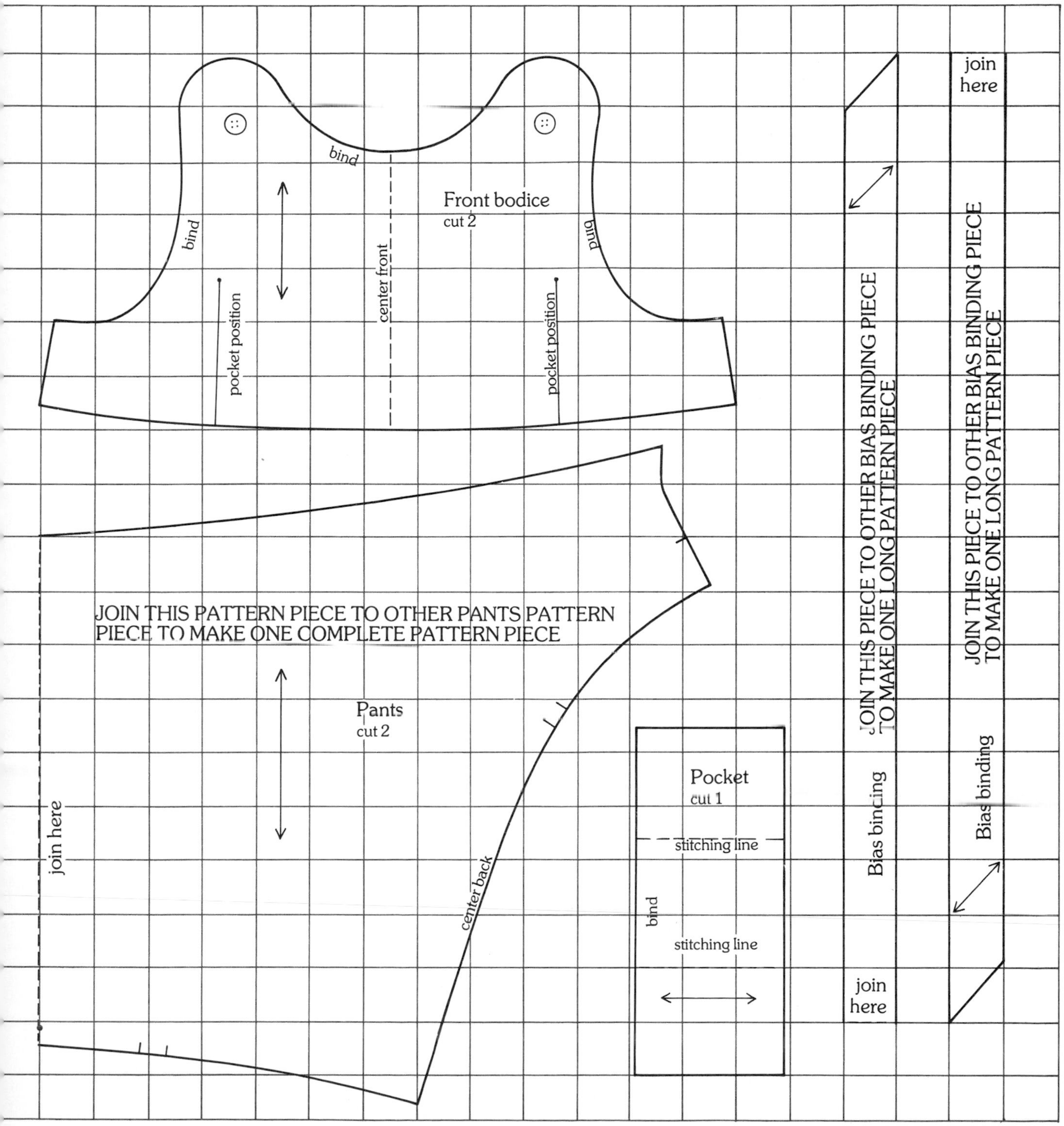

Front bodice
cut 2

bind

bind

bind

center front

pocket position

pocket position

JOIN THIS PATTERN PIECE TO OTHER PANTS PATTERN
PIECE TO MAKE ONE COMPLETE PATTERN PIECE

Pants
cut 2

center back

join here

Pocket
cut 1

stitching line

bind

stitching line

join here

JOIN THIS PIECE TO OTHER BIAS BINDING PIECE
TO MAKE ONE LONG PATTERN PIECE

JOIN THIS PIECE TO OTHER BIAS BINDING PIECE
TO MAKE ONE LONG PATTERN PIECE

Bias binding

Bias binding

join here

join here

SLEEP SUIT

You will need

For a sleep suit to fit a baby age 6 months to 1 year

1½yd of 36in-wide fabric or ⅞yd of 54in-wide soft, machine washable fabric such as stretch jersey or acrylic fleece
1⅛yd of narrow elastic
8in by 12in piece of medium-weight fusible interfacing
Motif
Thread

Designed for maximum comfort, this one-piece sleep suit will keep a baby warm in or out of bed.

A one-piece sleep suit is ideal for nightwear, as it cannot ride up and expose bare skin to the cold. This design has elasticized wrists and ankles, a long center zipper for easy dressing, set-in sleeves and a simple collar. ⅝in seam allowances are included throughout unless otherwise specified.

Making the pattern and cutting out

Enlarge the pattern pieces from the graph pattern below. Check the fit of the front and back pattern pieces and adjust the length if necessary along the lines indicated on the pattern.

Pin the pattern pieces to the fabric, following the cutting layout on page 128. Cut out. Transfer all pattern markings.

Sewing the seams and inserting the zipper

Place left front and back pieces right sides together and pin, baste and stitch side seams from underarm to lower edge. Repeat with right front and back pieces. Press seams open.

With right sides together, match raw edges of left front and back pieces along inside leg. Pin, baste and stitch from crotch to lower edge. Repeat for right front and back pieces. Press seams open.

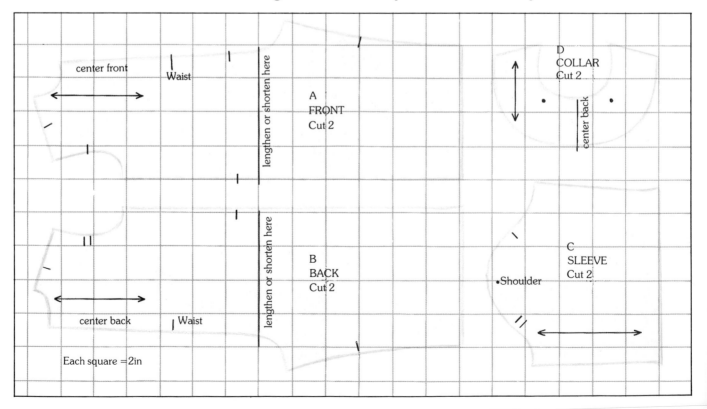

Turn one leg right side out and insert inside the other, so inside leg seams match. Pin and baste center back seam from neck, through crotch, to notch on center front seam. Stitch. Press seam as stitched. Baste center front seam from notch to neck edge. Press seams open.

Place closed zipper face down on center front seam allowances, placing stop just above stitched seam and aligning zipper teeth with basted seam. Pin in place and baste ¼in from center front. Stitch each side from base of zipper to neck edge, repositioning zipper foot as needed. Finish ends carefully and remove basting stitches.

Match back and front pieces at shoulders and stitch shoulder seams right sides together. Press seams open.

Setting in the sleeves

Fold sleeves in half, right sides together and stitch seams. Press seams open and finish edges. Turn sleeves right side out and thread through armhole so right sides are together. Pin in place, matching sleeve seam to side seam at underarm and dot at center of sleeve head to shoulder seam. Baste in place. Stitch with sleeve on top. Press seam as stitched and zig-zag raw edges together.

Making the collar

Cut interfacing to fit collar, trim away seam allowances on interfacing and fuse to wrong side of collar. Pin collar and collar facing together, right sides together, baste and stitch around outer edges. Trim corners, grade seams and clip curves. Turn collar right side out and press.

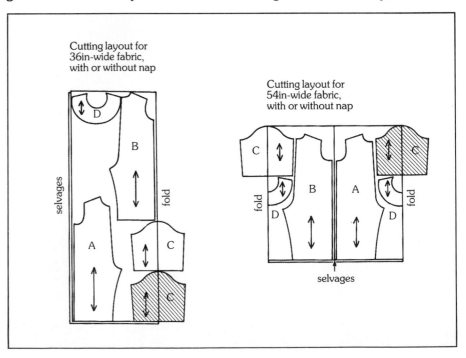

Pin neck edge of collar facing and neck edge of garment right sides together, matching dots on neck edge of collar to shoulder seams. Stitch, grade seam allowances and press seam toward collar. Slip stitch collar to garment.

Finishing

Zig-zag raw edges at wrist and ankles. Make a folded casing by turning ¾in to wrong side and stitching ⅝in from folded edge, leaving an opening to insert elastic. Topstitch ⅛in from folded edge. Insert elastic using a safety pin. Overlap ends by ½in and sew firmly together. Slip stitch opening closed.

Pin motif in position on one side of front. Baste around edges and stitch in place using a short zig-zag stitch.

LACY COLLECTION

You will need

For a shawl 45in square, and a dress, angel top and matinee jacket to fit 3 to 6 months or 19 to 20in chest
Fingering yarn:
14oz for shawl
3½oz for dress
3½oz for angel top
3½oz for matinee jacket
One pair each of sizes 7, 4, 3 and 2 knitting needles
Three small buttons for dress
Three small buttons for angel top
Four small buttons for matinee jacket

Gauge

30 sts to 4in over pat worked on size 4 needles

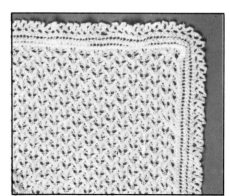

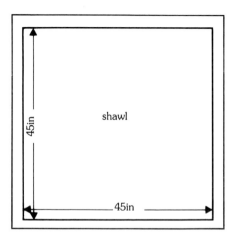

shawl

45in

45in

A hand-knitted collection like this, in a pretty, lacy stitch, is always a welcome gift.

The angel top, dress and matinée jacket have a yoke that is worked all in one piece, eliminating the need for any bulky seams.
A list of the abbreviations used is given on page 5.

Shawl

Using size 7 needles, cast on 243 sts. Beg lace pat as foll:
1st row (RS) K2, *sl 1-K1-psso, K3, yo, K1, yo, K3, K2 tog, K1, rep from * to last st, K1.
2nd row P2, *P2 tog, P2, yo, P3, yo, P2, P2 tog tbl, P1, rep from * to last st, P1.
3rd row K2, *sl 1-K1-psso, K1, yo, K5, yo, K1, K2 tog, K1, rep from * to last st, K1.
4th row P2, *yo, P2 tog, P7, P2 tog tbl, yo, P1, rep from * to last st, P1.
5th row K2, *yo, K3, K2 tog, K1, sl 1-K1-psso, K3, yo, K1, rep from * to last st, K1.
6th row P3, *yo, P2, P2 tog tbl, P1, P2 tog, P2, yo, P3, rep from * to end.
7th row K4, *yo, K1, K2 tog, K1, sl 1-K1-psso, K1, yo, K5, rep from * to end, ending last rep K4 instead of K5.
8th row P5, *P2 tog tbl, yo, P1, yo, P2 tog, P7, rep from * to end, ending last rep P5 instead of P7.
First-8th rows form lace pat and are rep throughout. Cont in pat until the 8th row of the 41 st pat rep has been worked. Bind off.

Edging

Using size 7 needles, cast on 11 sts. Knit one row. Beg edging pat as foll:
1st row K3, (yo, sl 1-K1-psso, K1) twice, (yo) twice, K1, (yo) twice, K1. 15 sts.
2nd row (K2, P1) 4 times, K3, (note that on this row each double yo is worked as 2 sts, the first being knitted and the second, purled). 15 sts.
3rd row K3, yo, sl 1-K1-psso, K1, yo, sl 1-K1-psso, K7. 15 sts.
4th row Bind off 4 sts, K4, P1, K2, P1, K3. 11 sts.
First-4th rows form edging pat and are rep throughout. Cont in pat until edging fits all around outer edge of main piece, allowing an extra 1½in at each corner and ending with a 4th pat row. Bind off.

To finish

Join cast-on and bound-off edging tog. Sew edging to main piece. Roll in a damp cloth. Lay flat, and leave to dry.

Dress (one piece to underarm)

**Using size 4 needles, cast on 243 sts. Work 7 rows in garter st (K every row). Work in lace pat as for shawl until dress measures 8½in from beg, ending with an 8th pat row.

Divide for armholes

Next row Work 63 sts in pat, bind off 2 sts, work in pat until 113 sts on right-hand needle after bound-off group for front, bind off 2 sts, work in pat to end.

Next row Work 61 sts in pat, work last 2 sts before bind-off tog, slip rem sts onto spare needle.

Keeping pat correct, dec one st at armhole edge on next 6 rows. 56 sts. Cut off yarn and leave sts on a spare needle.

With WS facing, rejoin yarn to front sts and, keeping pat correct, dec one

st at each end of next 7 rows. 99 sts. Cut yarn; leave sts on spare needle. With WS facing, rejoin yarn to rem sts and complete to match right back, reversing shaping. Do not cut off yarn, but leave sts on spare needle.**

Sleeves (make 2)

Using size 2 needles, cast on 40 sts. Work 3 rows in garter st.

Next row K4, *inc in next st, K2, rep from *to last 3 sts, K3. 51 sts. Change to size 4 needles. Work 8 rows in lace pat, inc one st at end of last row. 52 sts.

Shape cap

Keeping pat correct, bind off 2 sts at beg of next 2 rows, then dec one st at each end of next 5 rows. 38 sts. Work one row. Cut off yarn and leave sts on a spare needle.

Yoke

Using size 3 needles and with RS facing, work sts on spare needles as foll:

Next row K6, (K2 tog) 25 times across left back; K2 tog, K34, K2 tog, across left sleeve; K4, (K2 tog) 45 times, K5 across front; K2 tog, K34, K2 tog, across right sleeve; (K2 tog) 27 times, K2 across right back, turn and cast on 6 sts for underflap. 192 sts.

Work 11 rows in garter st.

Next row (buttonhole row) K1, K2 tog, yo, K3, *K1, K2 tog, rep from * to last 6 sts, K6. 132 sts.

Work 11 rows in garter st.

Next row (buttonhole row) K1, K2 tog, yo, K3, *K1, K2 tog, rep from * to last 6 sts, K6. 92 sts.

Work 7 rows in garter st.

Next row, K7, *K2 tog, K1, rep from * to last 7 sts, K7. 66 sts.

Next 2 rows K11, turn, sl 1, K to end.

Next 2 rows K22, turn, sl 1, K to end.

Knit one row across all sts.

Next 2 rows K11, turn, sl 1, K to end.

Next 2 rows K22, turn, sl 1, K to end.

Change to size 2 needles. Work 5 rows in garter st making buttonhole as before. Bind off loosely.

To finish

Join sleeve and underarm seams. Join back to underflap. Sew down underflap. Sew on buttons. Do not press; block if desired as for shawl.

Angel top (one piece to underarm)

Work as for dress from ** to **.

Sleeves (make 2)

Using size 2 needles, cast on 32 sts. Work 3 rows in garter st.

Next row K6, *inc in next st, rep from * to last 7 sts, K7. 51 sts.

Change to size 4 needles. Work in lace pat as for shawl until sleeve measures 5½in from beg, ending with an 8th pat row and inc one st in last row. 52 sts.

Shape cap

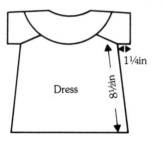

Dress

8½in

1¼in

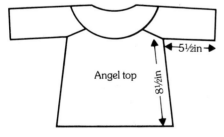

Angel top

8½in

5½in

Keeping pat correct, bind off 2 sts at beg of next 2 rows, then dec one st at each end of next 5 rows. 38 sts. Work even for one row. Cut off yarn and leave sts on a spare needle.

Yoke

Work yoke and finish as for dress.

Matinée jacket (one piece to underarm)

Using size 4 needles, cast on 243 sts. Work 7 rows in garter st. Work in lace pat as for shawl, working 6 sts at each end on every row in garter st until jacket measures 7in from beg, ending with an 8th pat row.

Divide for armholes

Next row K6, work 57 sts in pat, bind off 2 sts, work in pat until there are 113 sts on right-hand needle after bound-off group for back, bind off 2 sts, work in pat to last 6 sts, K6.

Next row K6, work 55 sts in pat, work last 2 sts before bind-off tog, slip rem sts onto spare needle.

Keeping pat and garter st border correct, dec one st at armhole edge on next 6 rows. 56 sts. Cut off yarn and leave sts on a spare needle.

With WS facing, rejoin yarn and, keeping pat correct, dec one st at each end of next 7 rows. 99 sts. Cut off yarn and leave sts on spare needle.

With WS facing, rejoin yarn to rem sts and complete to match left front, reversing shaping. Do not cut off yarn, but leave sts on spare needle.

Sleeves (make 2)

Work as for sleeves of angel top.

Yoke

Using size 3 needles and with RS facing, work sts on spare needles as foll:

Next row K1, K2 tog, yo, K3, (K2 tog) 23 times, K4 across right front; K2 tog, K34, K2 tog across right sleeve; K4, (K2 tog) 45 times, K5 across back; K2 tog, K34, K2 tog across left sleeve; K4, (K2 tog) 23 times, K6 across left front. 192 sts.

Work 11 rows in garter st.

Next row (buttonhole row) K1, K2 tog, yo, K3, *K1, K2 tog, rep from * to last 6 sts, K6. 132 sts.

Work 11 rows in garter st.

Next row (buttonhole row) K1, K2 tog, yo, K3, *K1, K2 tog, rep from * to last 6 sts, K6. 92 sts.

Work 7 rows in garter st.

Next row K7, *K2 tog, K1, rep from * to last 7 sts, K7. 66 sts.

Next 2 rows K to last 11 sts, turn, sl 1, K to last 11 sts, turn.

Next 2 rows Sl 1, K to last 18 sts, turn, sl 1, K to last 18 sts, turn.

Next row Sl 1, K to end of row.

Change to size 2 needles.

Work 5 rows in garter st making buttonhole as before. Bind off loosely.

To finish

Join sleeve and underarm seams. Sew on buttons. Do not press, but block if desired as for shawl.

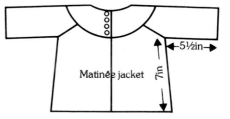

Matinée jacket

5½in

7in

SWAN LEGGINGS

You will need
For leggings to fit 3[6:12] months or 19[20:22]in chest
Sport yarn:
5[6:7]oz in main color MC (blue)
Small amount in contrasting color A (white)
One pair each of sizes 3 and 5 knitting needles
Eight small buttons

Gauge
24 sts and 32 rows to 4in over st st worked on size 5 needles

Make these practical leggings in a machine washable wool or cotton yarn. They can be worn over a tee shirt or sweater.

The stockinette stitch leggings are made in two pieces – back and front. Worked in single ribbing, the adjustable straps are worked separately and sewn to the front bib along the shaped edge. The straps cross over at the back and button in place. The ribbed button and buttonhole bands are worked last and sewn to the side openings from the waist to the underarm.

Figures for larger sizes are in brackets []; where there is only one set of figures, it applies to all sizes.

A list of the abbreviations used is given on page 5.

When working from chart use a separate ball of yarn for each color area worked, twist yarns tog on WS at joinings to avoid making a hole and where necessary strand yarn loosely across WS of work over not more than 5 sts at a time to keep fabric elastic.

Back
Legs (make 2)
Using smaller needles and MC, cast on 21[23:25] sts.
Beg K1, P1 rib as foll:
1st rib row (RS) K1 *P1, K1, rep from * to end.
2nd rib row P1, *K1, P1, rep from * to end.
Rep these 2 rib rows twice more and then the first row again.
Next row (inc row) Rib 1[2:3], *make one by picking up horizontal loop before next st and working into the back of it – called make one (M1) –, rib 1, M1, rib 2, rep from * to last 2[3:4] sts, M1, rib to end. 34[36:38] sts.
Change to larger needles and work even in st st until leg measures 9[9½:10¼]in from beg, ending with a WS row.
Leave sts on a spare needle and make 2nd leg in the same way.
Body
With RS facing and using larger needles and MC, K across 34[36:38] sts of first leg, cast on 7[7:9] sts for crotch, K across 34[36:38] sts of 2nd leg. 75[79:85] sts.
Work 3[3:5] more rows in st st, so ending with a WS row.
Dec one st at each end of next row and then every 4th row until 67[71:75] sts rem.
Work even in st st until back measures 2½[3:3½]in from crotch, ending with a WS row.
Mark each end of last row with a colored thread.
Bind off 3 sts at beg of next 2 rows. 61[65:69] sts.
Work even in st st until back measures 5¾[6¼:6¾]in from crotch, ending with a WS row.**
Shape back
Cont in st st, shaping back as foll:
1st and 2nd rows Work to last 28 sts, turn.
3rd and 4th rows Work to last 21 sts, turn.

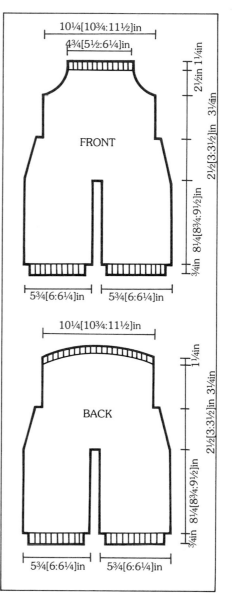

5th and 6th rows Work to last 14 sts, turn.
7th and 8th rows Work to last 7 sts, turn.
9th row K to end.
10th row P across all sts.
Change to smaller needles and work 10 rows in K1, P1 as for legs.
Bind off loosely in rib.

Front
Work as for back to **
Place motif
Beg charted motif on next row as foll:
1st pat row K15[17:19], work in pat across 31 sts of first row of chart reading chart from right to left, K15[17:19].

2nd pat row P15[17:19], work in pat across 31 sts of 2nd row of chart reading chart from left to right, P15[17:19].

Shape bib

Cont to work chart until the 18 rows are complete *and at the same time* shape bib as foll:

Keeping chart correct, bind off 3 sts at beg of next 6 rows.

Next row (RS) K1, K2 tog tbl, work in pat to last 3 sts, K2 tog, K1.

Next row K1, P2 tog, work in pat to last 3 sts, P2 tog tbl, K1.

Rep last 2 rows once more, keeping pat correct.

Next row K1, K2 tog tbl, work in pat to last 3 sts, K2 tog, K1.

Next row K1, work in pat to last st, K1.

Rep last 2 rows twice more. (Chart is now complete.) 29[33:37] sts.

Using MC only, work even in st st for 2[4:4] rows.

Change to smaller needles and work 10 rows in K1, P1 rib as for legs. Bind off loosely in rib.

Straps (make 2)

Press pieces lightly on WS with a warm iron avoiding ribbing. Join leg and side seams to markers.

Using smaller needles and MC, cast on 9 sts and work in rib as foll:

1st rib row K1, *K1, P1, rep from * to last 2 sts, K2.

2nd rib row K1, *P1, K1, rep from * to end.

Rep these 2 rib rows until strap, when slightly stretched, fits along one shaped edge of front bib. Sew in place and cont to work in rib until strap measures 10¼[10½:11]in or ½in less than required length, ending with a 2nd rib row.

Next row (buttonhole row) Rib 3, K2 tog tbl, yo, rib to end.

Cont in rib for 6 more rows. Bind off in rib.

Work 2nd strap in the same way.

Buttonbands (make 2)

Cast on and work in rib as for straps until band, when slightly stretched, fits up side of back from markers to bound-off edge of ribbing. Bind off in rib. Sew band to back. Work 2nd buttonband in the same way and sew to back. Mark positions for 3 buttons on the buttonband, the first and 3rd ¼in from either end and 2nd in the center.

Buttonhole bands (make 2)

Work as for buttonbands, but making buttonholes on rows to match markers as foll: Rib 3, K2 tog tbl, yo, rib to end.

To finish

Sew buttonhole bands to sides of front between markers and top edge of strap. Sew buttonhole and button bands tog along lower edges and sew to main piece along bound-off edge at markers.

Sew on buttons to correspond with buttonholes on sides. Sew 2 buttons to back ribbing so that straps cross over at back.

31 sts

key

⊠ = A

☐ = MC

RIBBED PANTS & CABLE TOP

This stylish, "preppy" outfit of a cabled top and comfy ribbed pants will be sure to put the wearer on the best dressed list!

No cable needle is needed for the simple cable pattern used on the top. The two-stitch cable crossover is made by knitting the second stitch on the left-hand needle and then the first before dropping both stitches from the needle. The lace effect at the center of the two-stitch cable is created by making a "yarn over" two rows after the cable is crossed and then dropping this extra stitch on the row before the next cable crossing. The stitches between the cable panels are worked in single ribbing.
Figures for larger size are in brackets []; where there is only one set of figures, it applies to both sizes.
A list of the abbreviations used is given on page 5.

Top

Back
Using size 3 needles and MC, cast on 60[71] sts.
Work in K1, P1 rib until ribbing measures ¾in.
Change to size 5 needles and beg pat as foll:
1st row (RS) *(K1, P1) 3 times, P1, K 2nd st on left-hand needle, do not slip off left-hand needle, but K into first st and slip both sts off left-hand needle at same time – called Cr2 –, P2, rep from * to last 5 sts, (K1, P1) twice, K1.
2nd row *(P1, K1) 3 times, K1, P2, K2, rep from * to last 5 sts (P1, K1) twice, P1.
3rd row *(K1, P1) 3 times, P1, K1, yo, K1, P2, rep from * to last 5 sts, (K1, P1) twice, K1.
4th row * (P1, K1) 3 times, K1, P3, K2, rep from * to last 5 sts, (P1, K1) twice, P1.
5th row *(K1, P1) 3 times, P1, K3, P2, rep from * to last 5 sts, (K1, P1) twice, K1.
6th to 9th rows Rep 4th and 5th rows twice more.
10th row *(P1, K1) 3 times, K1, P1, drop next st from left-hand needle and pull work sideways to release st, P1, K2, rep from * to last 5 sts, (P1, K1) twice, P1.
First-10th rows form cable pat and are rep throughout.
Work even in cable pat until back measures 11½[12¼]in from beg.
Bind off.

Front
Work as for back until front measures 9[9¾]in from beg, ending with a WS row.
Shape neck
Next row Work 30[35] sts in pat, bind off 0[1] st, work in pat to end.
Next row Work 28[33] sts in pat, K2 tog, turn leaving rem sts on a spare needle.

You will need
For pants and top to fit 3 to 6 [9 to 12] months or 19 to 20 [21 to 22]in chest
Sport yarn:
5[6]oz in main color MC (white)
5[6]oz in contrasting color A (blue)
One pair each of sizes 3, 5 and 7 knitting needles
Waist length of ½in-wide elastic

Gauge
25 sts and 31 rows to 4in over cable pat worked on size 5 needles
22 sts and 30 rows to 4in over K1, P1 rib worked on size 7 needles

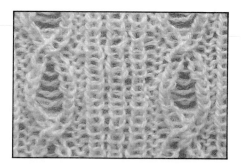

BACK

10¾[11½]in

¾in

9¾[11¼]in

2¾[3½]in   4¼in   2¾[3½]in

2½in

FRONT

8¼[9]in

¾in

9¾[11¼]in

Next row (RS) Work in pat to end.
Keeping pat correct, cont to dec one st at end of WS rows until there are 17[22] sts. Work even in pat until front measures same as back to shoulder.
Bind off.
With WS of rem sts facing, rejoin yarn at neck edge and complete as for first side, reversing shaping.

Sleeves (make 2)
Using size 3 needles and MC, cast on 29[32] sts.

Work in rib as for back until ribbing measures ¾in.
Change to size 5 needles and beg cable pat as foll:
1st size only
1st row (RS) K1, *P2, Cr2, P2, (K1, P1) twice, K1, rep from * to last 7 sts, P2, Cr2, P2, K1.
2nd size only
1st row (RS) P1, K1, *P2, Cr2, P2, (K1, P1) twice, K1, rep from * to last 8 sts, P2, Cr2, P2, K1, P1.
Cont in pat, inc one st at each end of next row and then every 4th row until there are 49[52] sts, working inc sts into pat. Work even in pat until sleeve measures 6¾[7½]in from beg. Bind off.

Neckband
Using size 3 needles and MC, cast on 110 sts. Work in K1, P1 rib until neckband measures 1½in. Bind off in rib.

To finish
Do not press. Join shoulder seams. Sew on sleeves with shoulder seam at the center. Join side and sleeve seams. Sew neckband around neck edge, then sew right edge of neckband to left side of neck opening in front.

Pants

Back
Legs (make 2)
Using size 3 needles and A, cast on 28[32] sts.
Work in K1, P1 rib for ¾in.
Change to size 7 needles and work even in K1, P1 rib until leg measures 7½[8¾]in from beg. Leave sts on a spare needle and make 2nd leg in the same way.
Shape crotch
Next row Rib 27[31] sts of first leg, work tog last st of first leg and first st of 2nd leg, rib to end. 55[63] sts.
Next row Rib 26[30] sts, work 2 sts tog, rib to end.
Work 4 more rows, dec one st at center of each row. 50[58] sts. Work even in rib until back measures 13[14¼]in from beg.
Change to size 3 needles and work in K1, P1 rib for 1½in. Bind off loosely in rib.

Front
Work as for back.

To finish
Do not press. Join side and inside leg seams. Fold waistband in half to WS and sew in place, leaving an opening for elastic. Cut elastic to correct waist size and insert into waistband and join the ends securely. Close opening. Turn bottom band of legs to RS and sew in place.

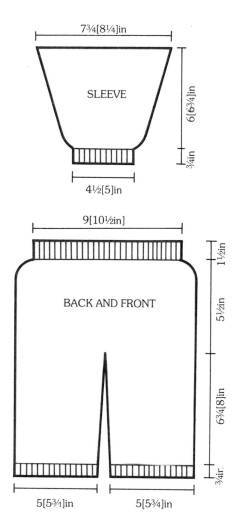

SLEEVE

7¾[8¼]in

6[6¾]in

¾in

4½[5]in

9[10½]in

1½in

5½in

6¾[8]in

BACK AND FRONT

¾in

5[5¾]in

5[5¾]in

LEGGINGS & CARDIGAN

You will need
For leggings and cardigan to fit 6 to 12 months or 20 to 22in chest
Sport yarn:
7oz in main color MC (pink)
5½oz in contrasting color A (white)
2oz in contrasting color B (pale green)
One pair each of sizes 2, 3 and 5 knitting needles
Three small buttons
Elastic thread

Gauge
20 sts and 36 rows to 4in over smocking pat worked on size 5 needles
24 sts and 30 rows to 4in over st st worked on size 3 needles

This classic set would also look good in yellow, white and pale blue or try a brighter combination for a more sporty outfit.

The cardigan is worked in a delicate, textured stitch. The leggings are knitted in stockinette stitch stripes with a bib in single ribbing.
A list of the abbreviations used is given on page 5.

Cardigan

Back
Using size 5 needles and MC, cast on 68 sts. Beg smocking pat as foll:
1st row Knit.
2nd row K1, *K1, knit into st below next st on left-hand needle and slip st off left needle – called K1B – rep from * to last st, K1.
3rd row Knit.
4th row K1, *K1B, K1, rep from * to last st, K1.
First-4th rows form smocking pat and are rep throughout.
Cont in pat until back measures 6¾in from beg, ending with a WS row.
Shape armholes
Bind off 7 sts at beg of next 2 rows. 54 sts.
Work even in pat until armhole measures 3½in, ending with a WS row.
Shape shoulders
Bind off 14 sts at beg of next 2 rows. 26 sts.
Leave rem sts on a spare needle for back neck.

Left front
Using size 5 needles and MC, cast on 34 sts. Work in pat as for back until front measures 6¾in from beg, ending with a WS row.
Shape armholes
Bind off 7 sts at beg of next row. 27 sts.
Work even in pat until armhole measures 2in, ending with a RS row.
Shape neck
Bind off 9 sts at beg of next row. Work one row.
Bind off 2 sts at beg of next row, work one row, bind off 2 sts at beg of next row. 14 sts.
Work even until front matches back to shoulder. Bind off.

Right front
Work as for left front, reversing shaping.

Sleeves (make 2)
Using size 3 needles and MC, cast on 31 sts. Work in K1, P1 rib for 5 rows.
Inc row Rib 4, (make one by picking up horizontal loop before next st and working into the back of it, rib 3) 9 times. 40 sts.
Change to size 5 needles and work in pat as for back, inc one st at each end of 5th row and then every 4th row until there are 60 sts.
Work even in pat until sleeve measures 7in from beg. Bind off.

To finish

Join shoulder seams. Match center of bound-off edge of sleeve to shoulder and sew in position, joining sides of sleeve to bound-off sts at underarm and easing in top of sleeve along armhole. Join side and sleeve seams.

Edging

With RS facing and using size 5 needles and B, pick up and K136 sts evenly around lower edge.

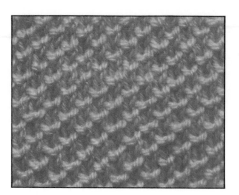

1st row (WS) Purl.
2nd row Knit.
3rd, 4th and 5th rows Purl.
6th row Knit.
7th row Purl.
Bind off loosely.
With RS facing and using size 5 needles and B, pick up and K44 sts evenly up right front, beg at hem row and ending at neck edge. Work as for lower edging, making buttonhole on first 2 rows as foll:
1st buttonhole row P2, bind off 2 sts, P to end.
2nd buttonhole row Knit, casting on 2 sts over those bound off on previous row.
Work left front edging as for right front edging, beg at neck edge, ending at hem row and omitting buttonhole.
With RS facing and using size 5 needles and B, pick up and K21 sts up right front neck, K26 sts from holder at back neck and pick up and K21 sts down left front neck beg and ending at hem row. 68 sts. Work as for lower edging. Sew hems to WS. Do not press. Sew on button.

Leggings

Back
Legs (make 2)
Using size 2 needles and A, cast on 33 sts. Beg ribbing as foll:
1st rib row K1, *P1, K1, rep from * to end.
2nd rib row P1, *K1, P1, rep from * to end.
Rep 2 rib rows until ribbing measures ¾in, inc one st in last row. 34 sts.
Change to size 3 needles and beg with a P row, work in st st for 6 rows.
Cont in st st, **work 1 row A, then, using MC, work eyelets across next row as foll:
Eyelet row (RS) K1, *yo, K2 tog, rep from * to last st, K1.
Cont in st st, working stripe sequence as foll:
1 row MC, 1 row A, 1 row MC, 2 rows A, 3 rows B, 2 rows A, 1 row MC, 1 row A, 1 row MC.
Using MC, rep eyelet row.***
Work 2 rows A, 3 rows B, 1 row A.**
Rep from ** to ** once.
Rep from **to *** once, so ending with a RS row.
Leave these sts on a spare needle and make 2nd leg in the same way.
Body
With WS facing and using size 3 needles and A, P across 34 sts of first leg, cast on 6 sts for crotch, P across 34 sts of 2nd leg. 74 sts.
Cont in st st, work 6 rows A.
*Using B, work eyelet row as for leg. Cont in st st, working as foll:
[1 row B, 1 row A] twice, 2 rows B, 1 row MC, 2 rows B, (1 row A, 1 row B) twice.*
Work 8 rows A.

Rep from * to *, using MC in place of B and B in place of MC.
Work even using A only until back measures 7¾in from crotch, dec one
st in last row. 73 sts.
Work in K1, P1 rib until ribbing measures 3¼in.

Shape armholes
Keeping to rib throughout, bind off 7 sts at beg of next 2 rows, 3 sts at
beg of next 2 rows, 2 sts at beg of next 2 rows.****
Dec one st at each end of next 6 rows. 37 sts.

Shape neck
Next row Rib 12, turn leaving rem sts on a spare needle.
Bind off 2 sts at beg of next row.
Work even on these 10 sts until shoulder strap measures 3¼in.
Dec one st at each end of next 2 rows. Bind off rem 6 sts.
Rejoin yarn to rem sts and bind off center 13 sts, work in pat to end.
Complete to match first side, reversing shaping.

Front
Work as for back to ****. 49 sts.

Shape neck
Work neck in rib as foll:
Next row K2 tog, rib 19, turn leaving rem sts on a spare needle.
Dec one st at neck edge on next row and then on every other row 4
times more, *and at the same time* dec one st at armhole edge on next
5 rows. 10 sts.
Work even on these 10 sts until front matches back to 2 rows before
bind-off.
Keeping rib correct, work buttonhole on next row as foll:
Buttonhole row Work first 2 sts tog, rib 1, work next 2 sts tog, yo, rib
3, work last 2 sts tog.
Dec one st at each end of next row. Bind off rem 6 sts.
Rejoin yarn to rem sts and bind off center 7 sts, work in pat to end.
Complete to match first side, reversing shaping.

To finish
Press pieces, foll instructions on yarn label.

Edging
With RS facing and using size 3 needles and A, pick up and K one st
from each row or st around front neck, beg and ending at center top of
shoulder strap and making sure there are an even number of sts.
Beg with a P row, work 3 rows in st st, so ending with a P row.
Next row K1, *K2 tog, yo, rep from * to last st, K1.
Next row Knit.
Beg with a K row, work 3 rows in st st. Bind off loosely.
Work edging along front armholes in the same way. Work edging on
back as for front. Joint edging seams at center of strap. Turn edging to
WS and sew down. Join side seams. Join inner leg seams and crotch.
Sew on buttons. Run elastic thread through ribbing at bottom of legs.

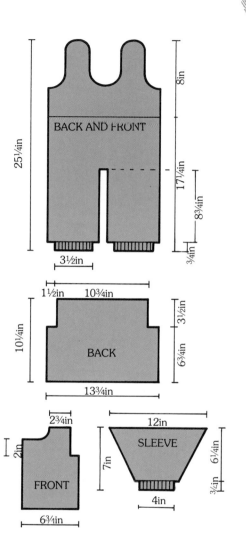

CROCHETED SHAWL

Crochet this beautiful pure white shawl for a new baby – it would make a welcome christening gift.

This shawl is crocheted using hairpin crochet. This is an old craft which was once worked on a hairpin. Today hairpin crochet is worked onto a special loom or fork, using a crochet hook, to form strips of loops. The loops are removed from the loom and joined. Single crochet edging and simple chain joining have been used for this shawl.
A list of the abbreviations used is given on page 5.

You will need
For a shawl approximately 42in square
13oz of a sport yarn
1in crochet loom
Size E crochet hook

Gauge
Each strip of hairpin crochet measures 1in in width with 22 loops to 4in worked on size E hook and 1in hairpin loom

To make
Strips (make 19)
Work first strip of hairpin crochet with sc worked in the center as foll:
Make a slip knot and place it on the right-hand prong with the bar of the loom at the bottom. Draw the loop out so that the knot is central between the 2 prongs and hold the yarn behind the left-hand prong. Turn the loom from right to left so that the yarn passes around the left-hand prong. Hold the yarn behind the prong as before. Insert the crochet hook through the left-hand loop, yo and draw a loop through, yo and draw yarn through loop on hook to complete first stitch at center. Keeping the loop on hook, lift the hook over the right-hand prong, so that it is behind the prong and turn the prong from right to left so that the yarn passes around the left-hand prong. *Insert the hook in the front of the loop on left-hand prong from front to back, and draw a loop through (2 loops on hook), yo and draw through both loops on hook to complete a single crochet in loop. Lift the hook over the right-hand prong, then turn the loom from right to left, so that the yarn passes around the left-hand prong.*
Rep from * to * until 220 loops have been worked on each side of strip, removing the loops from the loom each time it is full and replacing the last 3 loops before continuing. Fasten off.
Work 18 more strips in the same way.

Double crochet edging
Edge each side of each strip of hairpin crochet with single crochet edging as foll: Place slip knot on hook, insert hook in first 2 loops on one side of strip, yo and draw a loop through 2 loops of strip (2 loops now on hook), yo and draw through 2 loops on hook – 1sc made –, *ch1, 1sc in next 2 loops on strip, rep from * to end. Fasten off.

Join strips
Join the strips tog with chain joining as foll:
Place 2 strips tog, join yarn with a sl st to first sc of first strip, ch5, 1sc in first sc of 2nd strip, *ch5, skip next sc on first strip, 1sc in next sc on first strip, ch5, skip next sc on 2nd strip, 1sc in next sc on 2nd strip, rep from * to end.

To finish
Weave in all loose ends. Press or block foll instructions on yarn label.

Shell edging

Join yarn with a sl st to first sc of a side with sc edging, ch1, *1sc in same sc, 1sc in next ch-1 sp*, rep from * to * along first side to corner, ch2, along 2nd side work ** (3sc in loop sp) twice, 5sc in ch-5 sp **, rep from ** to ** along this side, ending with (3sc in loop sp) twice, ch2, work 3rd side as for first side and 4th side as for 2nd side, join with a sl st to first sc. Do not turn at end of rounds.

2nd round Ch1, *1sc in each st along side edge to corner, (1sc, ch2, 1sc) all in ch-2 sp at corner*, rep from * to * along rem 3 side edges, join with a sl st to first sc.

3rd round *Sl st in each of next 3 sts, 3dc in same st as 3rd sl st*, rep from * to * to corner, rep from * to * into ch-2 sp at corner, work rem 3 side edges in the same way, join with a sl st to first sl st. Fasten off.

146

CHRISTENING GOWNS

Make the christening a day to remember! This chapter includes a dazzling array of heirloom-quality christening gowns, any of which is beautiful enough to pass down to generations of the family. The gowns can be accessorized with a matching bonnet, delicate bootees and a lacy shawl (such as the knitted shawl on page 130 or the shawl worked in hairpin crochet on page 144).

The gown and bonnet on page 148 are the most traditional, trimmed with old lace and embroidered tulle. The basic designs are simple, but you can make them as ornate as you wish with trimmings.

Also styled along old-fashioned lines is the gown on page 153, which is based on a Victorian petticoat design. The eyelet and ribbon trim gives it a fresh, crisp look.

A more modern but equally delicate christening gown is the one on page 158, which features dainty appliquéd flowers. A shorter version of this makes a very pretty dress for any special occasion, as you can see from the cover photograph.

Finally, for those who enjoy embroidery, the beautiful gown on page 162 has intricately embroidered yoke and sleeves in a seasonal motif. You can choose the motif to match the time of year of the baby's christening, thereby marking the occasion in a very special way.

LACY GOWN & BONNET

This basic christening gown and bonnet can be left plain and simple or decorated in a variety of beautiful ways.

The christening gown consists of full sleeves and a skirt gathered onto a yoke; the bonnet has a main section that is gathered onto a crown. This simple design offers a wide choice of decorative possibilities. It could, for example, be made up in a combination of fabrics or be embellished with embroidery. The gown and bonnet in the photograph combine muslin and pieces of old lace and embroidered tulle. The skirt has a front panel, and fine tucks are worked by machine across the skirt. Lace trims the neck edge, wrists, skirt hem and lining hem, and a lace ruffle decorates the edges of the yoke. Ribbon rosettes are sewn onto the skirt, and lace edging together with ribbon rosettes and streamers are added to the bonnet. Many embroidery stitches and techniques can be used to achieve a delicate and pretty effect. (Remember, however, that incorporating too many elements in one garment can create an over-complicated, fussy look.)

½in seam allowances are included throughout unless otherwise specified.

Cutting out

Enlarge the yoke, sleeve and bonnet pieces from the graph pattern shown on page 151, and cut out. For a plain skirt cut a piece of fabric measuring 44in wide by 24in long. For a skirt with a front panel cut two pieces, one measuring 30in wide by 24in long for the main skirt and one piece measuring 14in wide by 24in long for the center panel. If the skirt is to have tucks allow ¼in for each ⅛in tuck on the skirt length.

Making the gown

If the fabric being used is marquisette, baste the dress yoke and sleeve pieces onto the silk lining and make them up as one fabric.

Run a gathering thread between the notches on the top of the sleeve. With right sides together, matching notches and drawing up the gathers evenly to fit, baste and stitch the sleeves to the yoke. Press the seam toward the yoke.

With right sides together, baste and stitch the underarm seams. Clip the curves and press the seams open.

With right sides together, baste and stitch the front skirt panel to the skirt. If the skirt is being made without a panel, make a seam up the center back of the skirt, leaving a 4in opening. For a skirt with a panel, make a center back opening on the main skirt piece by cutting a 4in slash. Finish the raw edges of the slash with a narrow hem.

If using skirt lining, sew it as described for the skirt (but without any tucks). With the right side of the lining facing the wrong side of the skirt, baste the lining to the skirt along the top edge.

Run a double line of gathering thread around the top edge of the skirt. With right sides together, matching the center front of the yoke and drawing up the gathers evenly to fit, baste and stitch the skirt to the yoke.

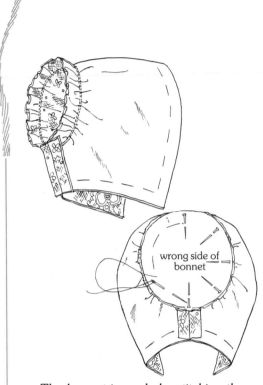

wrong side of bonnet

The bonnet is made by stitching the two main sections together then gathering around the back (top). The main section is then stitched to the crown (above). The front and neck edges are bound and finally the bonnet is trimmed. Stages in making the gown (below): the yoke facing, lace-trimmed sleeve edge and completed back opening.

With right sides together, baste and stitch the yoke facing to the yoke, making ¼in seams around the neck and down the back opening. Clip the curves and turn the yoke right side out. With the right side facing, baste around the center back and neck opening, rolling the seam to the wrong side to give a smooth line. Press the basted edges. Turn the seam allowance on all edges of the yoke facing to the wrong side. Baste and stitch the yoke facing to the yoke at the stitching line along the top of the skirt and around the armholes. Press on the wrong side.

Make a narrow hem on the sleeve edge and sew on the lace trimming. Run two rows of shirring elastic, threaded double in the needle, along the lines indicated on the graph pattern.

Make a narrow hem on the skirt and, with right sides together, sew on the 4in-wide lace trimming (optional). Press lace to hang down.

If using skirt lining, make a narrow hem on it. (The lining should be 1in shorter than the skirt.) Sew the lace trimming onto the hem of the lining.

Slightly gather the lace trimming and sew it around the neck edge. Sew buttons to the neck opening as shown and make loop buttonholes on the opposite side.

Making the bonnet

If using marquisette, baste the marquisette and lining together for the crown piece and the main section of the bonnet, and treat as one fabric.

With right sides together, baste and stitch the center back seam of the main section. Run a double row of gathering thread around the back of the main section as indicated on the pattern. Draw up the gathers, adjust them evenly and with right sides together, stitch the main section to the crown. Finish the front and neck edges with 1in-wide bias binding cut from the fabric. Trim around the crown and the front edge with slightly gathered ½in-wide lace. Sew the ribbon rosettes and streamers in position on the bonnet.

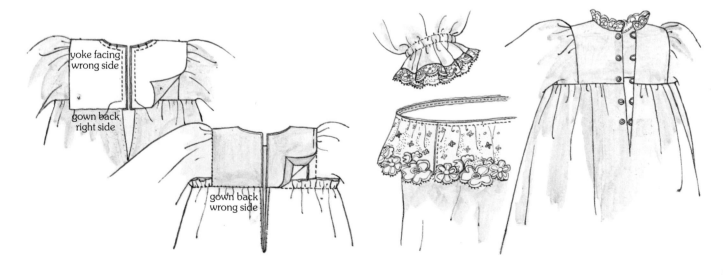

yoke facing wrong side

gown back right side

gown back wrong side

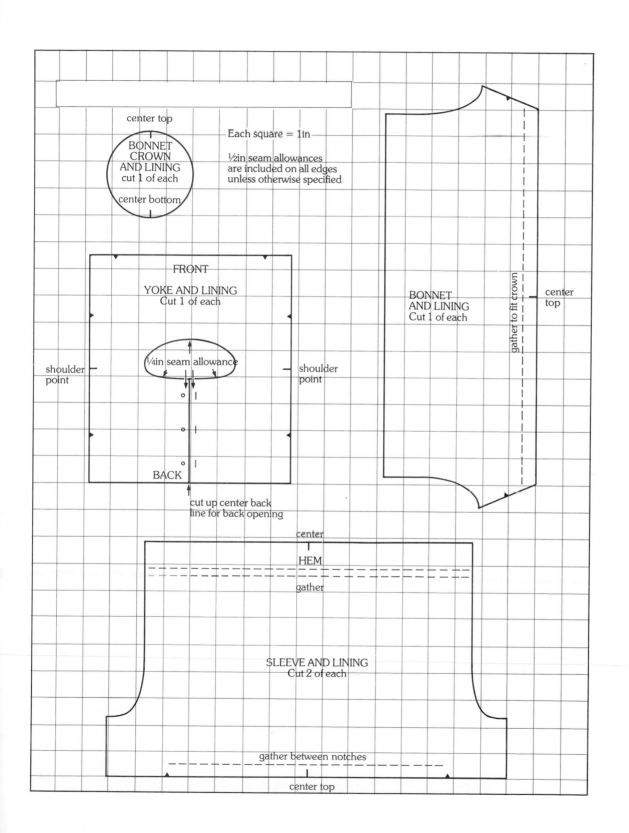

center top

BONNET
CROWN
AND LINING
cut 1 of each

center bottom

Each square = 1in

½in seam allowances
are included on all edges
unless otherwise specified

FRONT

YOKE AND LINING
Cut 1 of each

¼in seam allowance

shoulder
point

shoulder
point

BACK

cut up center back
line for back opening

BONNET
AND LINING
Cut 1 of each

gather to fit crown

center
top

center

HEM

gather

SLEEVE AND LINING
Cut 2 of each

gather between notches

center top

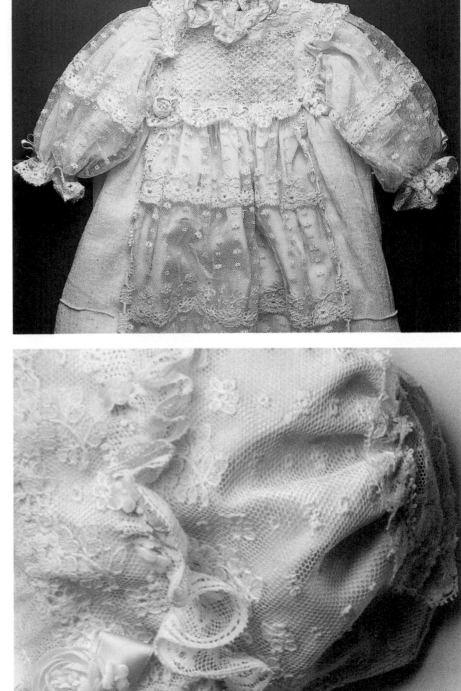

Detail of the bodice (above right) reveals embroidery on net combined with machine-made lace. A variety of stitches and techniques can be used on a christening gown like this — for example, satin stitch, French knots or shadow work. One way to adapt the pattern would be to make it from tulle and embroider it as shown in the illustration above. The bonnet too can be varied — the detail on the right shows the ribbon and lace edging used on this bonnet.

RIBBON-TRIMMED GOWN

The pretty tucks and delicate trimming on this christening gown will make it a family treasure.

This exquisite christening gown for a three to six month old baby is inspired by a Victorian petticoat design. The basic shape is very simple, consisting of a skirt gathered onto a yoke, but the tucks, satin ribbon, eyelet and feather stitching give it special charm. For a winter christening, use a wool/cotton mixture; for a summer christening, a fine lawn or muslin. A lining will be necessary if the fabric is transparent.
⅝in seam allowances have been included throughout unless otherwise specified, and French seams are used throughout.

Making the yoke
The tucked yoke sections are prepared before the pattern pieces are cut out. For the front yoke, cut a piece of fabric 15¾in by 5½in. For the back yoke, cut two pieces of fabric each 8in by 5½in. Mark tuck lines on the yoke pieces as indicated in the diagram on page 157. These lines are the stitching lines. Fold halfway between the first pair of lines, wrong sides together, and stitch through both layers of fabric to form a ¼in tuck. Repeat for the other tucks. Press each group of tucks outward.
Cut out paper patterns for the front and back yoke sections following the measurement diagram and cutting layout shown on page 155. Fold front yoke, matching tucks. Pin pattern piece on fabric and cut out. For the back yoke, pin the two pieces of fabric together around edges, matching tucks. Position the pattern piece over the two yoke pieces and cut out.
Stitch front yoke to back yokes at shoulders. Turn under and baste 1⅛in-wide facings at center back, finishing edges. Overcast neck edge. Cut two 8in lengths and one 3in length of eyelet beading. Cut two 8in and one 3in lengths of ribbon and thread through the eyelet beading. Topstitch the short length between the tucks on the center front yoke. Topstitch the longer lengths close to armholes over shoulders. Cut two 4in lengths of ribbon and stitch in place between the second and third tuck, each side of the center front. Stitch one edge of the ribbon only, stitching close to the tuck stitching line.
Cut a length of ⅝in-wide border eyelet or lace edging to fit around neck edge, adding 1¼in allowance for finishing each end. With raw edges even, stitch edging around neck. Finish edges.

Making the skirt
Measure and cut out the back and front skirt sections, following the measurement diagram on page 155. Place center front on fold of fabric. Cut two back pieces. Use flexible curve to draw in underarm shape. Mark lines for three horizontal tucks, each ¼in deep as shown. Mark center back opening.
Stitch side seams of skirt and center back seam as far as opening.
Turn up and stitch a 2½in hem.

You will need
For a gown measuring 33in in length, to fit a 3-6month old baby
2 ⅛yd of 36in-wide fabric (or 4¼yd of 36in-wide fabric if the gown is to be lined)
Thread
5yd of ⅜in-wide satin ribbon
2¼yd of ¼in-wide satin ribbon
2¾yd of ⅝in-wide lace or eyelet beading (designed to be threaded with ribbon)
2½yd of ¾in-wide lace edging or border eyelet
2¼yd of 1½in-wide lace edging or border eyelet
Two ⅜in-diameter buttons
Stranded cotton embroidery floss (optional)

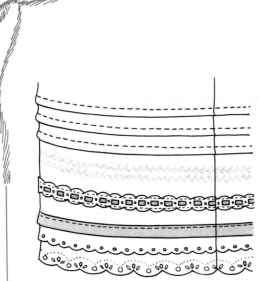

The lower edge of the christening gown features tucks, feather stitching, lace beading with ribbon threaded through it, ribbon trim and eyelet.

Measurement diagram

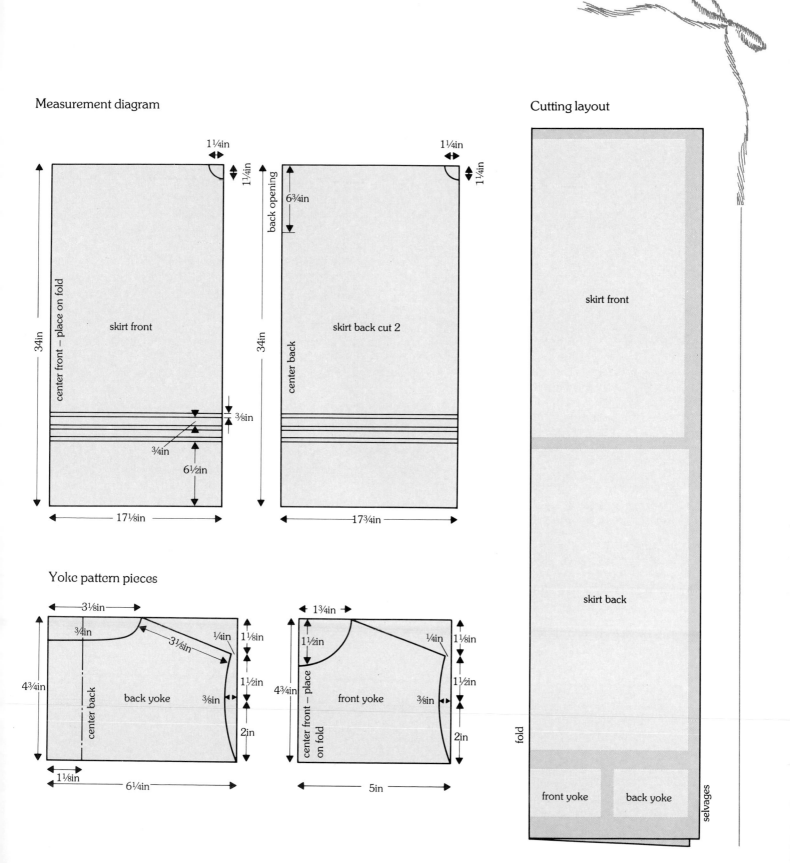

skirt front

center front – place on fold

34in

1¼in

1¼in

¾in

6½in

17⅛in

back opening

6¾in

skirt back cut 2

center back

34in

1¼in

1¼in

17¾in

Yoke pattern pieces

3⅛in

¾in

3⅛in

¼in

1⅛in

4¾in

back yoke

center back

⅜in

1½in

1⅛in

6¼in

2in

1¾in

1½in

¼in

1⅛in

4¾in

front yoke

center front – place on fold

⅜in

1½in

5in

2in

Cutting layout

skirt front

skirt back

fold

front yoke

back yoke

selvages

155

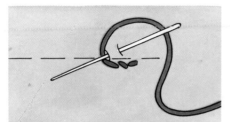

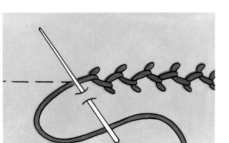

To embroider feather stitch, mark the positions of the two lines of feather stitch with lines of basting. The stitch is worked from the right side of the fabric, from right to left. Fasten the thread with a tiny backstitch on the wrong side of the fabric, on the line of basting. Bring the needle to the right side of the fabric. Take a small stitch diagonally above and to the right, bringing the needle over the marked line and looping the thread around it (top). Make the second stitch below the line, taking a small diagonal stitch and looping the thread around the needle as before (above). The stitches should be about ⅛in apart, 1/16in away from the marked line, on alternate sides of the marked line.

Decorating the skirt

Stitch three horizontal tucks, ¼in deep, around hem of gown in positions marked. Cut 69in lengths of the following: ¾in-wide border eyelet or lace edging, 1½in-wide border eyelet or lace edging and ¼in-wide lace or eyelet beading. Cut two 69in lengths of ribbon, and thread one length through lace or eyelet beading.

Pin and baste the wider border eyelet or lace edging around the hem, starting from the center back seam so that the edge just covers the hem of the dress. Pin and baste the narrower border eyelet or lace on top, raw edges even, so that it overlaps. Turn under and finish the ends of the edging at center back. Make one row of stitching through the top edges of the two pieces.

Pin and baste one length of ribbon over the raw edges of the border eyelet or lace edging. Stitch on upper edge only, finishing ends as before. Thread the remaining length of ribbon through the lace or eyelet beading. Pin, baste and stitch in place above ribbon so that the hem stitching is covered, finishing ends as before.

Work 2 rows of feather stitch around the skirt, between the top of the hem and the first pin tuck, marking the positions of the lines first with basting.

Sewing yoke to skirt

Run two lines of gathering stitches around top edge of skirt. Pull up threads until skirt fits lower edge of yoke. Pin yoke to skirt, right sides together and raw edges matching, distributing gathers evenly. Baste and stitch in place. Press seam allowances up.

Finishing the gown

Make a ¼in hem around armholes and center back opening from the waist downward. Sew two buttonholes, one ¾in from the top of the bodice and the other 2in below that, on the righthand side of the bodice opening. Sew two buttons to the lefthand side to match. Stitch two ¼in-wide ribbons, each 40in long, in place on either side of front at base of yoke, and tie in a bow.

Lining the gown (optional)

If you are using a transparent fabric it will be necessary to line the gown. In this case, make up the lining without decoration.

Tucks for yoke pieces

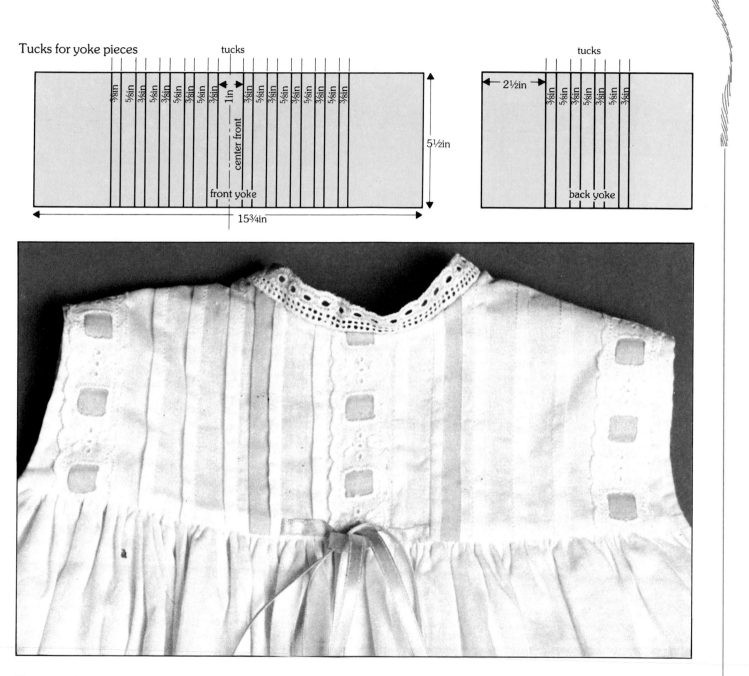

tucks

3/8in 5/8in 3/8in 5/8in 3/8in 5/8in 3/8in 5/8in 3/8in 1in 3/8in 5/8in 3/8in 5/8in 3/8in 5/8in 3/8in 5/8in 3/8in

center front

front yoke

5½in

15¾in

tucks

2½in

3/8in 5/8in 3/8in 5/8in 3/8in 5/8in 3/8in

back yoke

Prepare the tucking for the yoke as described and cut out. Then cut out a second, plain yoke. Baste yoke and lining together and then make up as one piece of fabric.

For the skirt, cut out a second skirt from lining fabric and stitch side and center back seams. Slip lining inside skirt with wrong sides together and baste along top edge. Gather up and stitch to yoke in one with the top layer. Stitch the lining hem separately, making a 3in-deep hem.

The yoke of the christening gown is decorated with tucks, eyelet and lace beading threaded with ribbon.

157

APPLIQUÉD GOWN

You will need

For a gown with a back length of 16½in
1¾yd of 54in-wide white cotton fabric
¼yd of 36in-wide apricot fabric
⅛yd of 36in-wide green fabric
1⅝yd of 1⅛in-wide eyelet
Green, white and apricot stranded cotton embroidery floss
White thread
4in by 16in rectangle of lightweight fusible interfacing
Two small white buttons

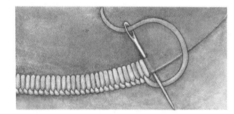

To embroider buttonhole stitch, bring the needle out of the background fabric by the edge of the appliqué. Insert the needle into the appliqué fabric above the edge, then take a downward stitch back to just beyond the edge. Loop the thread under the point of the needle and pull the needle through, tightening the loop. Repeat all around the edge of the shape.

To work a broad, twisted stem stitch bring needle up at beginning of line. Take it forward and re-insert it a little to the right of the line, keeping the thread to the right of the needle. Bring the needle up again halfway along the first stitch and slightly to the left, ready for the next stitch. Continue with even stitches to the end of the line. To produce a strong, narrow line, always bring the needle up and re-insert it along the line itself.

Combine appliqué with embroidery to make a dainty christening gown – or a pretty, short dress for any special occasion.

This pretty appliqué design is based on heart and leaf shapes, combined with the simplest embroidery stitches. The heart shapes on the yoke pattern are slightly smaller than those on the skirt, but the leaf shapes are the same on both.

⅝in seam allowances are included throughout unless otherwise specified.

Cutting out

Enlarge the pattern pieces for sleeve, front yoke and back yoke from the graph pattern on page 160. Trace the skirt pattern and extend as indicated. Cut out all pattern pieces from the white cotton except one front yoke, making sure the grain on the pattern lies on the grain of the fabric. For the remaining front yoke to be appliquéd, cut a piece of fabric 16in by 8in.

Working the appliqué

Trace pattern on page 160 for the yoke appliqué and transfer it to the center of the rectangle of fabric, using dressmaker's carbon paper.

Cut the interfacing in half and fuse the pieces to the wrong side of the green and apricot fabric. Transfer the small heart shape to the wrong side of the apricot fabric twelve times, and the larger heart twenty times. Transfer the leaf shape to the wrong side of the green fabric 24 times. Allow sufficient space between motifs for cutting.

Cut out a small heart shape and pin and baste in position on the white yoke fabric. Embroider closely all around in buttonhole stitch, using one strand of apricot embroidery floss and starting and finishing stitching at the point of the heart. Repeat with other small hearts until all the petals are in place.

Embroider stem stitch in apricot embroidery floss on the lines between flowers, then embroider a small circle in satin stitch (see page 51) using two strands of white floss in the center of each flower.

Cut out a leaf shape and baste in place on the design. Work all around in close buttonhole stitch in green floss. When the entire design is complete, press lightly from the wrong side over a soft towel. Place yoke pattern in the center over appliqué and cut out the yoke pattern piece. Trace the pattern for the skirt appliqué from page 160 and transfer it to the center of the skirt piece with the lowest flower 2¾in from the bottom edge. Embroider the design in the same way as that on the yoke.

Making the gown

Join center back seam to within 4¾in of top edge. Press seam open and finish raw edges. Turn under the raw edge on the seam allowances of the open section and hem in place. Turn under a narrow double hem all around bottom edge of gown. Baste eyelet to wrong side of bottom edge and feather stitch (see page 156) in place all around. Make a fold ⅝in from the bottom edge all around and work running stitches ⅛in

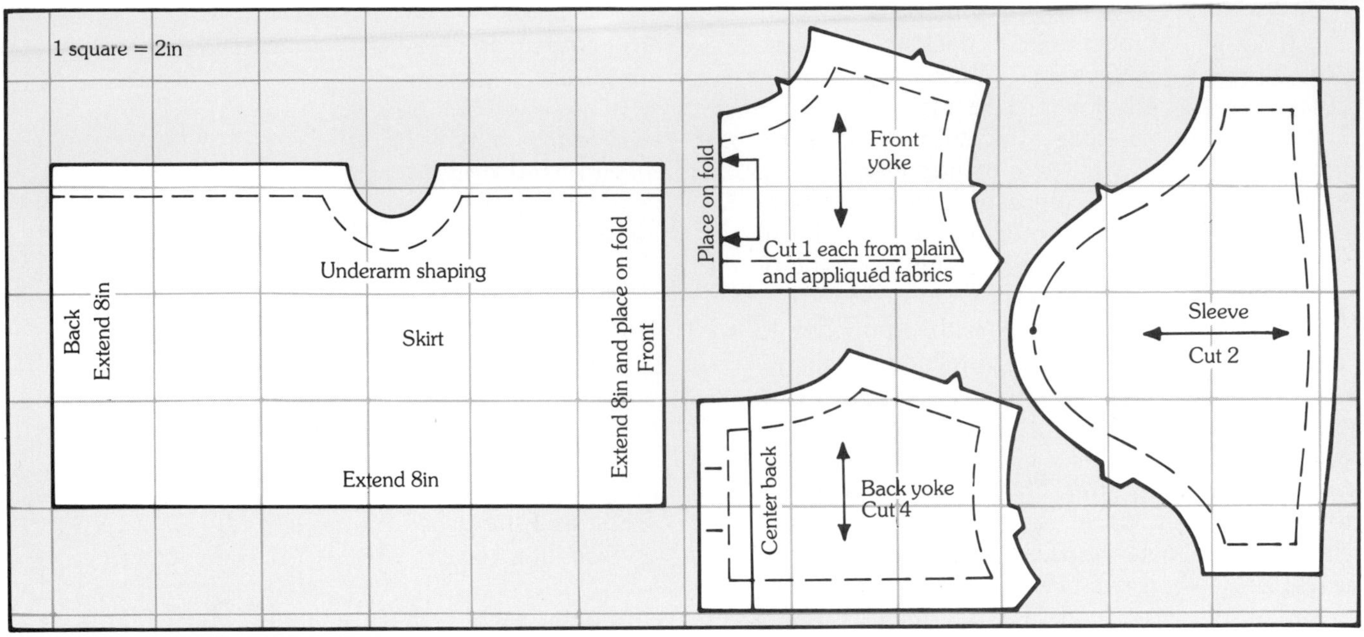

1 square = 2in

Underarm shaping

Skirt

Back
Extend 8in

Extend 8in

Extend 8in and place on fold
Front

Place on fold

Front
yoke

Cut 1 each from plain
and appliquéd fabrics

Center back

Back yoke
Cut 4

Sleeve
Cut 2

*Shown above, small heart and pattern
for yoke appliqué. Below, larger heart,
half of the pattern for skirt appliqué (to
be repeated in reverse), and the leaf
shape common to both yoke and skirt.*

from the fold. Make two more tucks in the same way at ½in intervals. Stitch appliquéd front yoke to back yokes at shoulder seams. Press open and trim seam allowances. Stitch plain front yoke to remaining back yokes in same way for yoke facing.

From remaining apricot fabric cut four strips 1¼in wide on the true bias for piping. Fold each piece in half lengthwise and stitch $\frac{1}{12}$in from the fold. Pin and baste a piece of piping all around neck edge so that the stitching on the piping is matched up with the stitching line on neck, and raw edges are together. Baste a strip of piping on stitching line of bottom of yoke on front and backs.

Place yoke and yoke facing with right sides together. Baste and then stitch, starting at yoke base seam line at back, going up one side of center back, around neck and down other side of center back to back yoke base. Trim seam allowances and clip curves. Turn right side out, baste in place and press.

Stitch a gathering thread along top edges of skirt. Baste and stitch skirt to yoke front and back. Trim seam allowances and press seam up. Piping should be enclosed in the seam. Turn under seam allowances on yoke facing and neatly catchstitch hem to the stitching line.

Setting in the sleeves and finishing the gown
Stitch a gathering thread around sleeve heads and set sleeves into armholes with right sides together and notches matching. Baste and stitch in place. Stitch a gathering thread around bottom edge of sleeves. Cut two strips 8in × 1½in from apricot fabric and, with right sides together, join short edges of each piece. Matching seams, baste and stitch sleeve bands to sleeves with right sides together. Trim seam allowances, turn under raw edges and slip stitch in place. Sew two buttonholes at the center back of garment and attach buttons to match.

This same pattern can also be used to make a very pretty dress, simply by shortening the skirt. The dress shown here has been made in an easy care polycotton.

EMBROIDERED GOWN

You will need

For a christening gown with a finished length of 34½in, to fit age 12 months:
2¾yd of 36in-wide white cotton lawn
2¼yd of 36in-wide green cotton lawn
One skein each Bates Anchor brand cotton embroidery floss in the following colors: white 0402, variegated green 1213 and variegated red 1204
10yd of ½in-wide white lace edging
1⅜yd of ¼in-wide white satin ribbon

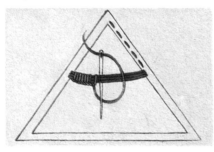

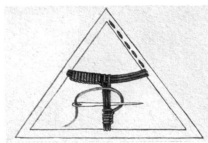

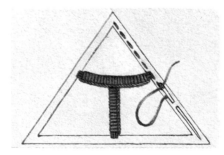

To work the buttonhole bars, first take two or three threads across from right to left and buttonhole back to the center. Take the same number of threads from the center down to the fabric below and buttonhole back up to the center. Work the buttonholing across to the starting point and continue running stitch around motif.

Make this delightful christening gown and embroider seasonal motifs on the yoke and sleeves.

The christening gown in the photograph, made from snowy white lawn with a green contrasting lining, is embroidered with colorful sprigs of holly. Other seasonal motifs are shown on pages 166-7. This type of embroidery, known as Richelieu embroidery, is a very decorative form of cutwork that's perfect for a christening gown.

As an alternative to a full-length gown, the skirt could be shortened and the sleeve embroidery omitted to make a special nightgown. Or you could shorten the sleeves and skirt to make a very pretty summer dress in plain or printed fabrics.

⅜in seam allowances are included on skirt, sleeve and ruffle; ¼in seam allowances are included on bias and all yoke sections.

Enlarging and transferring the pattern

Enlarge the pattern pieces from the graph pattern on page 164. Cut out. Press the fabric to remove all wrinkles. Place the pattern pieces in position and, with pins or tailor tacks, mark out the gown sections. Embroider the yoke and sleeves before cutting out and sewing.

Working the embroidery

To transfer the motifs, place the lawn over the holly leaf trace pattern on page 166, matching the straight grain to the center line. Using a medium-hard pencil, trace the motifs through. Stretch the fabric in a 10in embroidery hoop.

Work the embroidery in one strand throughout. Following the colors given, first work the spider webs and all the connecting bars in buttonhole stitch. Next, buttonhole the holly motifs, then the outline.

Buttonholing is done by first working two rows of running stitch just inside the double lines of the design, then working buttonhole stitch (see page 158) over the double lines. Buttonhole bars are worked as shown on this page and spider webs as shown on page 165. Remember to keep the twisted edge of the stitch facing the area which will later be cut away, and avoid stranding across the back.

Using small, sharp-pointed embroidery scissors, carefully cut away the areas of background fabric. First make initial cuts from the right side, cutting across the center of the area into any points. Turn work to wrong side and carefully cut away fabric, as near to the buttonhole edge as possible. Stroke any remaining threads of background fabric up and away from the edge before trimming.

Press the embroidery on the wrong side.

Cutting out

Replace the pattern pieces on the fabric and cut out each section. Cut out the appropriate lining sections from the contrasting fabric. Cut a bias strip of white lawn 1in by 7in for the neck binding.

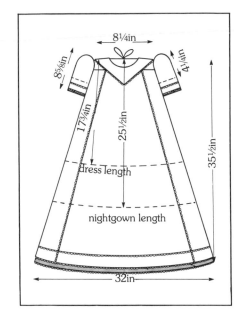

Making the yoke

With the straight grain and notches matching, place the right side of the green fabric under the front and back yoke sections. Pin and baste around the edges. Sew the two side sections to the yoke front with ¼in seams. Stay stitch ¼in away from the neck edge on all three pieces. Finish the unnotched edges of the yoke backs, turn in on the fold line and press to the inside to form facings. Baste around the neck edge in order to hold the layers in place.

Making the front and back

Working on the wrong side, face the front with the green panel placed between the notches. Make ¼in seams on the long sides and baste in place. Working on the right side, apply lace trim to the seam lines. Sew gathering stitches along the upper edge between the armhole seams. Repeat for the two back sections. Turn under ¼in on the back opening and stitch to finish.

Attaching the yoke

Working on the wrong side, pin the front to the yoke front matching center notches. Pull up the gathers to fit, baste and stitch, avoiding the point of the yoke. Press the seams upward. On the right side, baste the point of the yoke neatly in position, over the gathers, and cover the seam with lace. Trim away the excess fabric under the point. Before repeating for the two back sections, open out the yoke facings. Finally, turn under ¼in on the lower edge, turn in and slip stitch facing to seam line.

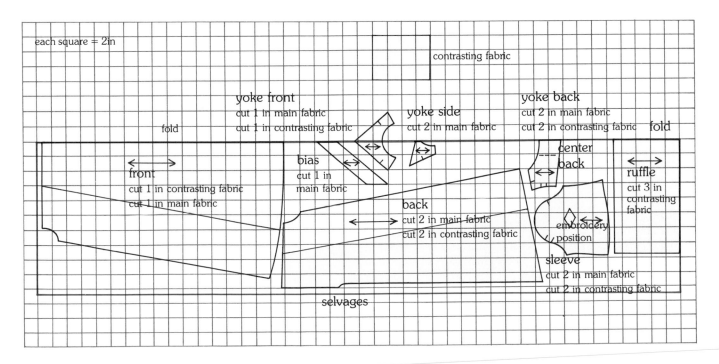

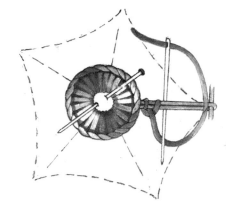

Binding the neck
With right sides together, stitch the shoulder seams. Baste and stitch the bias strip to the neck edge with a ¼in seam and leaving the short ends extending. Turn in the ends and fold the bias strip over the raw edge to the wrong side. Turn under ¼in and baste in place over the previous stitch line. Neatly slip stitch to finish.

Preparing the sleeves
For each sleeve turn under ¾in on the wrong side on the wrist edge of both fabrics. Place the green fabric behind and baste as before. Sew a line of gathering stitches between notches on each sleeve top. Apply lace to the outer edge and a second row 1in above.

Setting in the sleeves
With right sides together, pin the sleeves in place, matching the dots at the shoulder seams. Pull up the gathers to fit. Baste and stitch between the side seams, easing the fullness. Stitch a second time, trim and press seam toward sleeve. Stitch the side and sleeve seams in one operation. Stitch center back seam to point marked.

Making and attaching the ruffle
For the contrasting ruffle, stitch the seams to form a circle. Turn a ⅛in hem to the right side and cover with lace. Gather the top edge into four manageable sections, and put to one side.
On the main garment, turn under and baste a 2in hem. Press fold and attach lace to the lower edge. On the wrong side, pin and baste the ruffle in place over the edge of the seam allowance, pulling up gathering to fit. Apply lace to the right side, using basting as a guideline. Finally, remove all basting and press.

Attaching the ribbon ties
To finish, attach three sets of ribbon ties, each one measuring 8in long, to the back opening. Tie into bows.

To work looped picots on a spider web, make the foundation ring by first winding the embroidery thread two or three times around a stiletto or knitting needle to the required size. Continuing with the same thread, buttonhole around and join the stitches to complete the ring. Keep the thread attached.

Pin the ring in place and make the first bar by picking up a small stitch on the outside edge of the web. Take the needle back to the starting point, pick up a stitch from the edge of the ring and continue to buttonhole the bar to the center without piercing the fabric underneath.

For the picot, pin through the fabric as shown. Take the thread under the pin head from left to right and up over the bar. Pass the needle downward behind the bar and pull through. Take through the loop on the pin and twist the thread once around the needle before pulling through. Pull the thread tight, remove the pin and finish the bar. Complete the spider web.

Here are three seasonal motifs which can be embroidered especially to suit the time of a new baby's christening. Use them as trace patterns for Richelieu embroidered yoke and sleeve head motif. Place under the center fold of the fabric before tracing through.

Winter roses
Red, white and yellow are perfect colors for embroidering this tiny crescent of wintry Christmas roses onto the dress yoke. Use a cheerful, bright red jap silk for the lining.

Autumn roses
Choose the soft, glowing colors of variegated thread shading through pale yellow to cinnamon to suggest the first touch of autumn. Use pale yellow batiste or silk for lining the yoke, sleeves and skirt panels.

Spring petunias
Embroider small clusters of flowers around the yoke using single strands of fairly vivid petunia colors. A sharp turquoise blue lining contrasts with the embroidery and turns the white lawn into a lovely spring blue.

167